JESUS
AND THE
MYSTERIOUS
GOSPEL
OF THE KINGDOM

*Can You See the Bird's Nest
in My Mustard Tree?*

ROGER H. GRUMMER

ARCHWAY
PUBLISHING

Unless otherwise indicated, all scripture quotations are from The Holy Bible, English Standard Version (ESV). Copyright 2001 by Crossway Bibles, a division of Good News Publishers. Used by permission. All rights reserved.

Archway Publishing books may be ordered through booksellers or by contacting:

Archway Publishing
1663 Liberty Drive
Bloomington, IN 47403
www.archwaypublishing.com
1 (888) 242-5904

Because of the dynamic nature of the Internet, any web addresses or links contained in this book may have changed since publication and may no longer be valid. The views expressed in this work are solely those of the author and do not necessarily reflect the views of the publisher, and the publisher hereby disclaims any responsibility for them.

Any people depicted in stock imagery provided by Thinkstock are models, and such images are being used for illustrative purposes only. Certain stock imagery © Thinkstock.

ISBN: 978-1-4808-4552-7 (sc)
ISBN: 978-1-4808-4553-4 (e)

Library of Congress Control Number: 2017904907

Print information available on the last page.

Archway Publishing rev. date: 04/03/2017

To Betty,
Who walks with me in the Lord,
and
Cheryl, Cynthia, and Jonathan

Contents

Acknowledgments

My thanks to my wife, Betty, for designing the front cover; and to Stella Hlad, who helped to prepare the manuscript for publication.

Preface

There are some passages of the Bible I wish would have included a more expanded explanation. *Jesus and the Mysterious Gospel of the Kingdom* is an inquiry into one of those portions. This inquiry has a more pastoral approach than an academic or scholarly one. As such, I hope the reader will discover that this arrangement of information can be in some way helpful in the development of one's faith formation.

I WAS WONDERING

HAVE YOU EVER wondered, like I have, what it was Jesus taught that was so appealing to those who heard him? If what Jesus proclaimed didn't enhance their lives, I doubt they would have continued to follow him. So maybe it wasn't that he was an especially handsome and charismatic speaker or even a great teacher. It may have been something more radically foundational about the message he proclaimed that favorably touched the innermost being of those who heard him.

A Bible passage triggered my interest into what it really was that Jesus taught. It says, "And he went throughout all Galilee, teaching in their synagogues and proclaiming the gospel of the kingdom and healing every disease and every affliction among the people" (Matt. 4:23–25). For me those words pose more tantalizing questions. What did Jesus mean by this "gospel of the kingdom"? This and other questions prompted me to inquire further into what this mysterious gospel of the kingdom was all about.

Of course, it was a different kind of world in which Jesus and his hearers lived. What those words mean to people today might be different from what they meant to people back then. Cultural differences could account for what people understood at the time of Jesus and how something might be understood for us today. There are also many similarities to what people were like at that time and what people are like now. It seems to me that human nature hasn't changed all that much over the centuries. On the other hand, many things other than human nature have, in fact, changed dramatically.

OTHER WORLDS

Astronomers are now discovering the existence of more and more planets that seem to be somewhat earthlike. Here on earth, I wonder how earthlike our planet is compared to when the earth was younger. Both the vastness of space and the extent of time challenge us to assess the similarities and differences that exist between the world now and the world at the time of Jesus. I'm sure my great-grandparents and those who lived before them would have stood in awe of the changes that have taken place since the time they were alive. Compared to our world today, I wonder how otherworldly the world would seem to those who lived at the time of Jesus.

To many of us, living during Jesus's time might seem quite challenging. Just imagine what life would be like without electricity, automobiles, airplanes, modern medical advances, computers, the Internet, and other conveniences we take for granted every day. Each day would be a challenge. Just before the most challenging times of his life, Jesus spoke with his disciples and said, "In the world you will have tribulation. But take heart; I have overcome the world" (John 16:33). Every day also presents us with challenges and opportunities; both are difficult. Challenge encounters difficulty we experience in the present. We recognize opportunity in the present as hope. That hope is anticipated as a fulfillment in the future. Of course, the difficulty of hope is that the reality foreseen in hope isn't yet experienced and is often pursued while following a challenging road. People living at the time of Jesus experienced much of the same challenges and opportunities we do today.

It was into a world of challenge and opportunity, hope and difficulty, that Jesus came. He came proclaiming the gospel of a kingdom, bringing hope and healing to a people who needed what he came to offer them. "Take heart," he said. He came to "overcome the world," (John 16:33) to offer them the experience of another world that was better than the one they experienced every day.

GOOD NEWS

It was good news to hear that someone could overcome the kind of world in which he or she lived. The Bible says Jesus proclaimed the *gospel* of the kingdom. That kingdom was a world much better than the world God's people seemed to be chained. The root meaning of the word *gospel* actually means "good news." I doubt very seriously that Jesus appealed to the crowds by telling them how bad they were and how they could expect more bad times in the future. He didn't tell them there was no hope for them either in this life or in a life to come. He didn't tell them God would forever hold their sins against them. He didn't come to condemn them to everlasting punishment in hell. Such a message wouldn't have been considered good news. Such a message would have hardly encouraged multitudes of people to come hear him. Jesus had a different message for the people.

He proclaimed not bad news but rather good news to a people who longed to hear a word of encouragement and hope. Yet that message he proclaimed seems rather mysterious. What was this gospel of the kingdom really all about?

The land where the Jewish people lived at the time of Jesus was a land dominated by successive foreign powers, including the Persians, the Greeks, Hellenistic Seleucids, Egyptians, and finally the Roman Empire. They had felt like an oppressed people for many years. They longed to live in a world of freedom, where they could worship without restraints and where their hopes and dreams could be realized without fear or without being crushed by the capricious dictates of a tyrannical government. They wanted a life of freedom where they could love and be loved, and where they could live peacefully and joyfully in the presence of their Creator. They yearned for the good news of the coming of the Messiah promised by their prophets of old—a Messiah who would set them free from the oppressive burdens they were experiencing.

It may seem strange that the gospel or good news Jesus proclaimed didn't sound like the gospel proclaimed in Christian churches today. Today the proclaimed gospel message tells us the good news of a promised Messiah who has come, a personal Savior who came in the person of Jesus to save us from the eternal consequences of our sins.

Did Jesus go throughout the countryside, proclaiming that his life, death, and resurrection would now save them from the dire consequences of their sins? He hadn't yet died. He hadn't yet risen from the dead. He didn't continually proclaim he was the Messiah. Yes, he did make this known (John 4:25–26), but he also told his disciples not to broadcast his messianic identity openly (Matt. 16:15–20).

Jesus is called the Son of God, which simply meant God was born as all human sons are born. Theologians know this process as "the incarnation." Jesus was actually God, who loved us so much that he came to earth, born as a human being, to free people not from tyrannical and evil earthly governments but from the eternal consequences of having offended God with our sinfulness. The good news is that Jesus, the Son of God, perfectly expressed the divine love to all people of every time and place through his life, suffering, and death on a cross. He even then demonstrated the truth of it all through his resurrection to life again. Jesus did all this for us so we could live with God as his loved children now in this life and even after we die. The Bible pretty much summarizes this good news in these words: "For God so loved the world, that he gave his only Son, that whoever believes in him should not perish but have eternal life. For God did not send his Son into the world to condemn the world, but in order that the world might be saved through him" (John 3:16–17).

As we mentioned, at the time Jesus proclaimed the good news, or the gospel of the kingdom, he hadn't yet suffered and died on a cross, nor had he risen from the dead. So the gospel Jesus proclaimed was necessarily expressed quite differently from how Christians generally express it today. Considering that the good news of the kingdom Jesus proclaimed must have necessarily been stated differently, I find myself intrigued. And at the same time, it does also seem rather mysterious. Just what was this mysterious gospel of the kingdom Jesus proclaimed?

You may be somewhat like me if you like good news and aren't too picky with the form in which it is delivered. Of course, the form chosen must not distort the news conveyed, but instead it must present the news in such a way that it faithfully remains good news. Jesus expressed the gospel of the kingdom in ways that may seem strange or even mysterious to us.

Chapter 2

THE KINGDOM

WHEN JESUS SPOKE about the good news of the kingdom, he spoke in terms everyone could understand. The Jewish people understood very well what kings and kingdoms were all about. They experienced how good or how bad it could be to live in a kingdom ruled by emperors or kings. Kings and kingdoms and princes and princesses were all familiar to me as a child from the many fairy tales and adventure stories I read. The world of fantasy was always fun, but in the real world, there were very few kings or queens. The royal families around the world were becoming fewer and fewer.

Those kingdoms that actually exist have never seemed to me to be as much fun as in the world of make-believe. Real-world monarchies and other nations of the world have their problems. The people in any nation or kingdom aren't always happy and content with their governments. People often strive in as many different ways as there are nations or kingdoms to change or improve their situations. Sometimes those strivings bring violence and war. People who live in difficult situations don't want more bad conditions; they instead want good news of something better.

To the Jewish people of his day, Jesus expressed the good news or gospel in terms of a kingdom. This accounts for the expression we previously quoted in the Gospel of Matthew, the gospel of the kingdom, which Jesus proclaimed. Think about it; even the word *kingdom* calls to mind that a king is associated with a certain domain, the king's domain, or simply the kingdom.

It may seem a little perplexing the way Jesus identified or used the term *kingdom*.

For me the use of the words *gospel of the kingdom* seems somewhat mysterious. In some places in the Bible where it mentions the kingdom, it is often identified as the kingdom of God or even as the kingdom of heaven. For a while I thought all these kingdom terms singularly applied to the heaven of the blessed in the afterlife. Later, I thought perhaps the kingdom may also refer to something more than a blessed afterlife. Then I came to the understanding that it was a custom, especially among the Jewish people (most of the early Christians were, of course, Jewish just as Jesus himself was).

The phrase "kingdom of heaven" was actually a kind of euphemism or linguistic circumvention to avoid using the name of God for fear of misusing his name. To misuse God's name would have been a violation of one of the Ten Commandments. Instead of saying the name of God, they at times substituted the word *heaven.* The "kingdom of heaven," then, meant the same as the "kingdom of God." So finally I concluded that for me, whether the expression is "kingdom of God" or "kingdom of heaven," we are basically talking about the same kingdom, even though there may be some theological nuances that might be made from time to time based on their usages.

In connection with the king and kingdom concepts, I remember that the Bible tells us about the time a man by the name of Nathanael was introduced to Jesus. Those who introduced him to Jesus had already come to the conclusion that Jesus could very likely be the messianic prophet Moses mentioned years ago (Deut. 18:15). Nathanael wasn't convinced. But when he met Jesus and Jesus revealed to Nathanael that he knew things about Nathanael others couldn't ordinarily have known, he was so impressed that he said, "Rabbi, you are the Son of God! You are the King of Israel!" (John 1:49).

That the first disciples of Jesus already identified him as the Son of God is remarkable. The expression "Son of God" isn't a designation indicating that the Son is somehow of lesser importance than God. The expression *Son* is simply a convenient indicator that we have one who is truly born as a man, a human. This is the belief that God became human through the process of being truly born as a human son of a human mother. Theologians refer to this process as the incarnation. He was God—that is, divine—and yet simultaneously truly a human being.

Nathanael called Jesus "king of Israel." In those days, a title like that was a messianic designation. The expression "king of Israel" is helpful to me in understanding what some Israelites at that time packed into the expression "king of Israel" and by extension how some may have understood that the king of Israel was being identified as a messianic figure sent by God. Of course, if we are speaking of a king, doesn't this also include the idea that the king is a ruler over a kingdom?

There is an account of Jesus appearing after his resurrection to two disciples, who walked along the road to the village of Emmaus. They had evidently heard that Jesus was found to be no longer in the tomb, but they couldn't yet fully comprehend that he had risen from the dead. As Jesus walked with them, they didn't at first recognize he was the risen Jesus, but they did speak about Jesus, saying, "We had hoped that he was the one to redeem Israel" (Luke 24:21). What may seem debatable is whether this remark at that time should be understood as revealing a hope that Jesus would redeem Israel from Rome and in this way bring into being the messianic kingdom or that this hope contained a more religious or spiritual hope for redemption from sin and its eternal consequences. One thing is certain: they had the hope that Jesus was a messianic figure, and messianic figures could bring in a new kingdom. Later that evening, "when Jesus was at table with them, he took the bread and blessed and broke it and gave it to them. And their eyes were opened, and they recognized him" (Luke 24:30–31).

Not all Israelites, however, viewed the understanding of messiah or something messianic in purely religious terms. Many, even among his close followers, understood the concept of messiah solely in the context of one who would deliver them from the oppressive rule of a foreign, pagan, military-political empire, such as the powerful Roman Empire, under whose rule they lived.

At any rate, whether the people understood the messiah would bring them deliverance in a religious sense or would deliver them from an oppressive earthly power, ushering in a new kingdom of freedom from oppression, just the fact that Jesus spoke about a kingdom would have immediately caught the people's attention. Kingdom talk would have been rather exciting good news to hear.

The thought of a better kingdom was good news to the people, because it was something that could greatly improve their lives. Fears could be relieved. Opportunities could be more easily envisioned. They could take heart and look forward to a real and better future for themselves and their children. Peace, confidence in living, and joy in the presence of God could be greater parts of their lives. Such a message would be welcome good news of the kingdom Jesus proclaimed.

EARLIER DREAMS OF A KINGDOM

It's almost as if the hopes and dreams of the Israelite people to have a kingdom of their own were part of their historical DNA. Centuries before the arrival of Jesus, leaders called "judges" ruled the Israelites. God selected and guided these judges to govern the people. This arrangement today would be called a "theocracy." God was their king, and the judges received the guidance they needed directly from God to lead the people.

In the Bible the book of Judges tells us about the acts of various judges. Some of the most well-known of the fifteen judges that led the Israelites were Deborah, Gideon, and Samson. At the time that the prophet Samuel ruled the Israelites, they began clamoring for a king so they could be more like the other kingdoms of the world. Samuel warned the people about having kings to rule them rather than judges. Having kings rather than judges to lead them was seen as an act of rejecting God as their king. To me it also sounds like the Israelites were trying to keep up with, or to be like, the other nations around them. It was, as we might say today, that they wanted to "keep up with the Joneses." To have a king like the other nations was their dream. They dreamed of being a real kingdom like the other kingdoms of the world. Their dreams could be in part a nightmare, as Samuel warned, which included burdensome taxes and slavery.

THE DAVIDIC KINGDOM

When Jesus proclaimed a message about a kingdom, understandably the ears of the people perked up with more than a little interest. It was as if the message of a kingdom struck a harmonic note with past desires of wanting a king to lead their very own kingdom. Not only that, but they also knew that in time they did finally get their king, King David.

King David was their hero king. He wasn't a perfect person. He was a murderer, an adulterer, and a sinful man among sinful men. But he led the nation toward greatness. In spite of all his faults, he was always portrayed as one who walked in the ways of the Lord. This was a designation of one who adhered to one God who was to be worshiped in one place—that is, Jerusalem. The land mass he brought under his control was larger than it had ever been. He set the stage for the building of a grand temple in Jerusalem. He could centralize the government and their religion as never before.

After the death of King David, his son Solomon continued as the king of Israel. He was characterized as the wisest and richest of all kings. The era of David and Solomon became known as a golden age of Israel. During the reign of Solomon, the temple David wanted to build was constructed. The nation became something all the people since then could take pride in. King David was also venerated because God said, "And your house and your kingdom shall be made sure forever" (2 Sam. 7:16). It is from the house of David, from his descendants, that the Messiah, the king of Israel, was to be found. When the Messiah would come to reestablish the Davidic dynasty, it would be a dream come true. The long-awaited kingdom could be whatever they imagined it could be. Such a kingdom could even be imagined as a little utopia they could call their very own.

The problem was that so many of the kings who followed David and Solomon were so wicked that some people very likely gave up on their dreams. Pagan rulers again took over the land. During the occupation of Antiochus IV, Epiphanes, the people experienced having their religious freedoms taken from them. Antiochus IV was nicknamed Epiphanes because he liked to think of himself and present himself as being somewhat of a god with grand powers. The term *Epiphanes* comes from a word in the Greek language of the Bible indicating that a person is showing forth one's self as godlike. He forbade the people to practice the ancient ceremonies and customs of their Hebrew religion. He desecrated their temple by making offerings to his pagan gods. He commanded the people to pay homage to an image of Zeus, which he placed in the temple area. They literally witnessed the eradication of their religion and culture, and the transformation of their nation into a copy of the pagan religion and culture of their powerful oppressors. What happened to them was eerily similar to what was described as happening to the people at the time of Nebuchadnezzar in the book of Daniel.

Finally, the people could take no more abuse. A priest by the name of Mattathias together with his sons, began an active revolt against Antiochus IV. Later his son Judas Maccabeus (nicknamed "The Hammer") took over the revolt. During his leadership of the revolt, the city of Jerusalem was victoriously taken under their control.[1] The temple and the altar were ceremonially cleansed.

The victory was celebrated for eight days, during which time the menorah in the temple miraculously remained lighted for all eight days, even though they had oil for only one day. The feast continued to be annually celebrated as the Feast of Dedication, the Feast of Lights, or Hanukkah, even to the present day. Jesus attended such a Hanukkah celebration, which is mentioned in the New Testament

(John 10:22–23). The revolt, often referred to as the "Maccabean Revolt," was finally successful in giving the people a nation—shall we say kingdom—which over time encompassed more territory than ever before. Judas Maccabeus, nor the succeeding Hasmonean rulers, was successful in bringing to the people the everlasting messianic kingdom they had hoped for.

Their claim to fame of finally securing a kingdom of their own didn't last long. Eventually the Caesars of Rome ruled the area, and Herod the Great was appointed king of Judea. In Herod the people had a king, but this king, like those of the Hasmonean state, wasn't a king of the Davidic dynasty. He was, in fact, an Idumaean, with allegiance to the Roman emperor. The Roman rule brought them more oppression, which in turn reignited and heightened the people's hopes for a messianic figure who could defeat the Romans and bring into fruition their long-held hopes for a kingdom of their own.

ZEALOTRY

To be zealous or passionate for some cause is often thought of as a desirable trait. To be enthusiastic about something seems to be much better than to be apathetic. On the other hand, it was surprising to me to learn that to be called a sports fan actually began as a nickname for a sports fanatic. To be called a fanatic seems to have a more negative connotation to me than to be called a fan. The same thing can be said about being a zealot. To have zeal or a passionate devotion to one's belief or faith can be seen as a desirable quality, but to be zealous in advocating extreme measures, including violence to achieve what one wants to accomplish, isn't so admirable.

There were those at the time of Jesus who lived under the Roman domination and were called "zealots."[2] They advocated doing anything they could, legal or illegal, to overthrow the Roman occupation. These zealots were revolutionaries who were willing to murder, cause violence of all kinds, and steal to finance their lawless activities. There were some, known as the "sicarii," who customarily carried a *sica* or dagger on their person so they might be ready for action at any time.[3] The government held a man by the name of Barabbas at the time the Roman governor Pilate interrogated Jesus. Barabbas could easily be called a zealot.

There was also one of the disciples of Jesus, named Simon, who was called "the zealot" (Luke 6:15). The Bible doesn't document that the disciple Simon was a zealot in the sense of an anti-Roman revolutionary. Possibly Simon was a zealot in the sense of being a devotedly zealous follower of Jesus. Many of the people, however, were so desirous of being liberated from their Roman oppressors that they looked to any figure, including someone of the revolutionary zealotry who might possibly be the hoped-for messiah of the Davidic dynasty, to lead them in defeating the Romans.

AN EXCURSUS

In connection with the association of the Messiah with David and the Davidic dynasty, it is an interesting side note that when Jesus was baptized, a voice came from heaven saying, "You are my beloved son; with you I am well pleased" (Mark 1:11). Today, names for children are often chosen because the name sounds good. Notice that the voice from heaven called Jesus "my *beloved* Son" (emphasis added). So many names in the Bible have meanings other than being merely a name that sounds good or a convenient way to identify people. For example, the name Abraham in the Hebrew language means father of a multitude, and the name Moses in the Hebrew language means to be drawn out, as in drawn from the water. The name *David* in Hebrew actually means beloved.[4]

When the voice from heaven (God) called Jesus "beloved," this event makes me wonder whether this could be making a veiled identification of Jesus with David and the house of David. It's like Jesus is being called "my Davidic son." If so, the voice from heaven (God) identified Jesus as the One who is God's Son and the continuation of, or the reappearance of, the Davidic kingdom. He was acknowledged as the promised king of Israel, the promised Messiah.

For me this declaration of the voice from heaven at the baptism of Jesus, which designated Jesus as God's Son, is by extension significant for me and my baptism as well. I believe that when I was baptized, I too was being identified as a son and child of God with the status of citizenship in his kingdom. This should be very good news for all baptized Christians. We Christians aren't just children of our earthly family; we are baptized children of God. We are now the royal children of the King. God loves me as one of his very own children. I like that fact very much.

DID JESUS PREACH THE GOSPEL OF THE DAVIDIC KINGDOM?

It seems strange to say that when the Bible tells us Jesus proclaimed the gospel of the kingdom, it is in effect saying that he was proclaiming the good news of the Davidic kingdom. This would especially be strange if what is meant by the Davidic kingdom is a kingship over a geographical territory with a political-military identification, as for example the Roman Empire or even like the previous Hasmonean state or the kingdom ruled by David and Solomon.

As you recall the words and actions of Jesus, a question comes to mind. Was his proclamation of the kingdom really centered on reviving or establishing an earthly empire, with armies and land conquests bringing together a wealthy economy and the ability to wield great power?

Didn't Jesus admit to the Roman procurator Pilate that he was a king? But then he explained, "My kingdom is not of this world. If my kingdom were of this world, my servants would have been fighting, that I might not be delivered over to the world" (John 18:33–36).

Clearly Jesus had in mind a kingship and kingdom quite different from what Pilate and many others at that time had in mind. It wasn't a kingdom fought for by the revolutionary zealots. It wasn't the physical, geographical, military, and political kingdom that would oppose and overthrow Caesar. The Davidic kingdom Jesus preached wasn't a kingdom of this world that would soon perish, as all kingdoms of this world do. It was a Davidic kingdom that wouldn't perish but would instead be established forever. God said to David, "I will raise up your offspring after you, who shall come from your body, and I will establish his kingdom. He shall build a house for my name, and I will establish the throne of his kingdom forever" (2 Sam. 7:12–16).

An incident took place during Jesus's ministry when the people decided he was the person who could give them everything they had ever wanted and that he certainly must be the messianic king they had hoped for. Jesus had just finished feeding five thousand people with five loaves of bread and two fish. The Bible tells us that after Jesus did this miraculous sign, they said, "'This is indeed the Prophet who is come into the world!' Perceiving then that they were about to come and take him by force to make him king, Jesus withdrew again to the mountain by himself" (John 6:14–15). Notice that the retreating action of Jesus speaks loudly that this wasn't the kind of messianic king he had come into the world to be. His actions said no to being drafted as a revolutionary, messianic king of this earthly world. It isn't any surprise, then, that when Pontius Pilate asked whether Jesus were a king that he responded that his kingdom wasn't of this world.

Although Pilate also may not have understood the reality of the kingship and kingdom associated with Jesus, he was still condemned to death on a Roman cross as a traitor or revolutionary insurrectionist against Caesar and the Roman Empire. He did indeed proclaim the good news of the Davidic kingdom, but not in the sense that most people understood. Not everyone saw or understood the whole truth of the Davidic kingdom that Jesus proclaimed. Just before Jesus ascended back into heaven his close disciples asked, "Lord, will you at this time restore the kingdom to Israel (Acts 1:6)?" They had been very closely associated with Jesus for approximately three years, and still it seems, even they did not fully see what Jesus meant by the kingdom. So, maybe we shouldn't feel too bad if we do not fully see what Jesus meant. The good news of the kingdom Jesus proclaimed indeed seems mysterious.

The very words and actions of Jesus refute the notion that he was a revolutionary messiah who would overthrow the Roman Empire and usher in a revived kingdom of Israel. Many understood this as the role the Messiah would play, but Jesus himself gave evidence that this wasn't his understanding of who he was. This wasn't the kind of messiah he was to be, and neither was it the kind of kingdom he came to proclaim. As the activity and words of Jesus are examined today, there are still those who continue to understand his role as Messiah to have included a renewed earthly kingdom despite Jesus's own rejection of that role and that kind of kingdom.

There is another role of Jesus some understood to be not only revolutionary but also apocalyptic. That his ministry was apocalyptic in nature includes the idea that it was his purpose to inform the people that God would soon bring about the end of the age. It is true that many people at that time believed the world was getting so wicked that the wicked ones deserved the judgment and just destruction God would bring about very soon at the close of the age. The Jewish sect of the Essenes, as revealed in the Dead Sea Scrolls, had such an apocalyptic world view.

To be sure, Jesus denounced worldly wickedness. Like John the Baptist, he called on people to repent because the kingdom of heaven was at hand. But such a message wasn't what I view as the complete good news of the kingdom. It was instead a message to help the people prepare their own hearts and lives to become part of the kingdom Jesus proclaimed.

The leaders of the temple, the temple establishment, did see Jesus as gaining a greater and greater following. They were aware that people thought of him in messianic terms. This became especially clear when reports of his preaching and healing ministry also included the raising of the dead. The temple establishment followed the ministry of Jesus and increasingly viewed him as being a counter temple leader, who was threatening their power and position. This opposition to Jesus was brought to a head, especially after Jesus raised Lazarus from the dead. "So from that day on they made plans to put him to death" (John 11:53). This plot against Jesus finally led to the crucifixion and death of Jesus.

A Paradisical Kingdom

The practice of the Roman leadership at that time was to affix a notice—the titulus—on the cross of execution, which explained the charge against the person being crucified. The inscription placed on the cross of Jesus read simply, "Jesus of Nazareth, the King of the Jews" (John 19:19).

Jesus, the King of the Jews, was crucified near two criminals who also hung on Roman crosses. One of the criminals said, "Jesus, remember me when you come into your kingdom." Jesus replied, "Truly, I say to you today you will be with me in Paradise" (Luke 23:42). Jesus called his kingdom a paradise. He was referring to the pleasurable experience of the afterlife. *Paradise* comes from an ancient Persian or Sumerian word that would have been used to identify a king's garden. I really like the "king's garden" understanding of the afterlife paradise Jesus mentioned. His usage of the word *paradise*, understood as a king's garden, fits so well with the descriptive notice of the titulus on the cross identifying Jesus as a king of the Jews. The vision of a lush and well-watered king's garden would also have been very appealing to the criminal on a cross and to the people living in the dry and rather arid region of Judea. It is also quite appealing even today to people who may think of their lives as rather harsh, dry, or unproductive.

Many often use *paradise* to reference the pleasurable location called the Garden of Eden in the Bible's creation narrative. The word *paradise* is also mentioned in two other places in the New Testament writings other than Jesus's mention of it while he hung on the cross. It is used in the sense of another heavenly dimension the apostle Paul mentioned in his second letter to the Corinthians 12:1–4. *Paradise* is also associated with the presence of God when it refers to the "tree of life which is in the paradise of God," mentioned in the Revelation to John 2:7.

The kingdom Jesus proclaimed from the cross fits not the description of an earthly kingdom with boundaries confined to this earth but rather the dimension related to the afterlife in the presence of God. The paradisical kingdom Jesus proclaimed seems to extend beyond earthly time and this finite dimension. His kingdom is much more extensive than time, space, and matter. Although earthly terms are necessarily used, obviously concrete, earthly terms cannot fully describe what this mysterious kingdom Jesus proclaimed is like.

Chapter 3

THE KINGDOM AND PRESENCE

TO KNOW GOD is present with me is an immense comfort and help, whether things seem to be going well with me or I am fearful and everything seems to be turning to dust. It is impossible for me to grasp much meaning regarding God's kingdom without recognizing the presence of God in that kingdom. That would be like apple pie without apples—empty and meaningless.

The presence of God among his people has always been of paramount importance. A passage in the book of the prophet Isaiah expresses that concept. He wrote, "Therefore the Lord himself will give you a sign. Behold, the virgin shall conceive and bear a son, and shall call his name Immanuel" (Isa. 7:14). These words of the prophet have been understood to refer to the Virgin Mary and the birth of Jesus. In the New Testament's Gospel of Matthew, we read, "'Joseph, son of David, do not fear to take Mary as your wife, for that which is conceived in her is from the Holy Spirit. She will bear a son, and you shall call his name Jesus, for he will save his people from their sins.' All this took place to fulfill what the Lord had spoken by the prophet: 'Behold, the virgin shall conceive and bear a son, and they shall call his name Immanuel (which means, God with us)'" (Matt. 1:20–23).

Jesus affirmed the importance of the presence of God with his people in the last chapter of the Gospel of Matthew, when just before his ascension he said to his disciples, "And behold, I am with you always, to the end of the age" (Matt. 28:20). It seems to me that the Gospel of Matthew makes a full circle of completion regarding the teaching of presence when it is brought to our attention in the first chapter of the Gospel using the name Immanuel, which means "God with us." Then, in the very last verse of the final chapter, Jesus completed the thought by saying he would be with us always, to the end of the age.

The importance of presence cannot be overstated. People need the presence of others. When God first created Adam, he said, "It is not good that the man should be alone; I will make him a helper fit for him" (Gen. 2:18). The theologian Paul Tillich wrote about the separateness and aloneness that exist among humans, even though they may have partners or experience the presence of others in a variety of ways. Of Adam and Eve he said, "They are each alone. The creation of the woman has not overcome the situation which God describes as not good for man. He remains alone. And the creation of the woman, although it provides a helper for Adam, has only presented to the human being who is alone another human being who is equally alone, and from their flesh all other men, each of whom will also stand alone."[1] Such is the aloneness the psalmist also spoke of when he prayed to God, "Turn to me and be gracious to me, for I am lonely and afflicted" (Ps. 25:16).

When we are experiencing difficult times, it is comforting to have a helper, a friend, or loved one present. This is also true regarding the joyful times we experience. People sometimes say things like, "I wish Mom or Dad or that certain person I love could be here to enjoy this with me." As a pastor, I often heard the words, "Thanks for being here, Pastor." For a number of years, I also served as needed as a hospice chaplain to the terminally ill. Most of the patients I called on were genuinely appreciative to have someone with them. Not everyone had others present who were close to him or her. I recall one such man, afflicted with AIDS, who was close to death but seemed so very alone without the benefit of the presence of family or friends. Death itself is truly a very individual and solitary experience, but being with a person who is dying seems for some in that hour to offer a comforting presence. Being with the dying person in prayer was certainly seen as important to him or her, but it was more than that; just being there personally also seemed to be exceptionally helpful and meaningful to him or her.

When a person dies, people often think, *I don't know what to say.* The words spoken can be comforting, but they are soon forgotten. What isn't forgotten is that you were present with him or her. It is good to be with people and to rejoice with those who rejoice and weep with those who weep.

One of the patients I spent time with during his last days was a World War II veteran. He was one of those many referred to as being one of the greatest generation. He experienced D-Day at the invasion on the beaches of Normandy. I listened ever so attentively as he described with teary eyes what it was like, as he put it, to be "crawling over dead bodies and bloody body parts" as he hit the beach. His wife, also in the room, later thanked me for being there; she mentioned that I was the first person he had ever talked to so extensively about that horrible experience. She said that after he told me about that experience, he seemed so much calmer and at peace. It was very soon after I was there with him that he died. It was good to have been given the privilege of sharing the presence of God with

him by being present with him at such an important time at the
end of his life.

There is a theology of presence that isn't often verbalized, and
perhaps it cannot always be expressed adequately with words, but all
of us must actualize it as we are present and interacting with others.
It is a monumentally significant part of living in the active presence
of God in his kingdom. The active presence of God with his people
is an integral part of the kingdom Jesus proclaimed.

When Jesus began his preaching ministry, he said, "Repent, for
the kingdom of heaven is at hand" (Matt. 4:17). When he said the
kingdom was at hand, I believe he included himself as making the
kingdom a present reality. It was like saying the kingdom is right
here before you, right now. The kingdom is here as I am present
with you, right here at hand. The kingdom is as close to you as my
fingertips. The kingdom is now appearing in person for you. Can
you see it?

SPEAKING ABOUT PRESENCE

Have you noticed that it's much easier to see how God was actively
present and working in your lives in the past? But as you are presently
going through the various experiences of your life, it isn't so easy to
see that he is currently present and working in your life. We can
certainly be encouraged as we see the active presence of God in our
lives in the past. During the present we bank on the truth that God
is still active in our lives, even though it is sometimes difficult to
recognize how he is active in our daily walk. When we are in the
kingdom, Jesus proclaimed that God is always at hand; he is always
present with us.

There is the story in the first book of the Bible about Joseph (Gen. 37–50). So many bad things happened in his life that it is a wonder that he not only survived but also continued through it all with his faith in God intact. As the second youngest of twelve brothers, he incurred their jealousy to such an extent that they plotted to kill him. He was thrown into a pit while they decided how to accomplish their plans.

Pits in the Holy Land are numerous. They occur naturally in limestone areas. Pits were often converted into cisterns. Other pits were frequently used as tombs. While Joseph was in the pit, a caravan of traders came through the land. His brothers sold him as a slave to the traders, who took him to Egypt. The brothers took Joseph's coat of many colors and soaked it with animal blood, reporting to his father that a wild animal had killed Joseph.

In Egypt Joseph was sold as a slave to a prominent Egyptian government official. There he worked very successfully as a house servant and was placed as an overseer of all the official's assets. Then the official's wife falsely accused him of sexual harassment because he wouldn't go to bed with her.

He was unjustly condemned to jail and spent quite some time in prison. He was such a model prisoner that he was soon placed in charge of all the other prisoners. While he was in prison, God gave him the ability to explain the meaning of dreams. He told the meaning of dreams for several of the prisoners. His talents were finally brought to the attention of Pharaoh, who had a disturbing dream, and he was released from jail to tell Pharaoh the meaning of his dream. Since Joseph had demonstrated remarkable talent in dream interpretation, Pharaoh was impressed, and Joseph was given a position of great responsibility equal to what today we would call a prime minister in Pharaoh's government. Obviously, God was actively present in Joseph's life.

The Bible is clear in respect to God's presence being with Joseph. It says, "Now Joseph had been brought down to Egypt, and Potiphar, an officer of Pharaoh, the captain of the guard, an Egyptian, had bought him from the Ishmaelites who had brought him down there. The Lord was with Joseph, and he became a successful man being placed in the house of his Egyptian master. His master saw that the Lord was with him and that the Lord caused all that he did to succeed in his hands" (Gen. 39:1–3).

At about this time, there was a great famine in the land of Joseph's father and brothers. They came to Egypt to buy grain. At this point they came in contact with Joseph, but they didn't recognize who he was. He could have easily had them arrested as spies, but instead he took care of their needs. He finally revealed himself to them as their brother. To their surprise, he forgave them of their misdeeds and said, "As for you, you meant evil against me, but God meant it for good" (Gen. 50:20).

Through all his troubles, Joseph continued to trust that God was actively present with him. The first Christian martyr, Stephen, spoke of Joseph and of how the presence of God was with him. He said, "And the patriarchs, jealous of Joseph, sold him into Egypt; but God was with him and rescued him out of all his afflictions and gave him favor and wisdom before Pharaoh, king of Egypt, who made him ruler over Egypt and over all his household" (Acts 7:9–10). In the New Testament, an expression used in 2 Corinthians 5:7 can also be applied to how Joseph survived and overcame all his difficulties and how we can do the same. "For we walk by faith, not by sight."

Those who live in the kingdom Jesus proclaimed live continuously in the active presence of God through good times and difficult days.

There is a saying that can easily be classified as a cliché, yet it is obviously true. It says that on dark and cloudy days, when the sun cannot be seen, we can be confident that it is still shining. Every day, no matter what we are experiencing, it is equally true that God is actively present with us. We may not always feel like God is present with us, but later, as we look back, like Joseph, we can often more easily see that God is always there to guide, direct, and empower us. Even when we are in the pits, dismissed as dead, wrongly accused, or unloved—or no matter what seems to be going against us—we can't see how God is present with us. It is still continually beneficial to have the faith that trusts he truly is with us and always actively supporting, empowering, guiding, and loving us to the end.

So it has been also with God's people throughout their history. When Jesus proclaimed the gospel of the kingdom to them, he was aware that he was speaking to a people most of whom were faithful and, even among those who were nominal Israelites, knew their historical heritage. They knew of Joseph and of how he'd brought his father and brothers to Egypt to save them. They knew that after a time in Egypt, they and their descendants became slaves. They knew how God through Moses freed them from slavery and brought them through the waters to a grand exodus that led them finally to the Promised Land. Most were familiar with Joseph's story because it was a prelude and part of the important Passover and Exodus history.

God was actively with them as they exited Egypt, and he led them with a pillar of fire and a pillar of cloud. He was with them as they sang and danced for joy at their freedom from slavery. Throughout the many hardships they experienced during their forty-year experience in the wilderness, God was with them. In the desert when they needed food and water, he provided them with water from a rock to drink and manna from heaven to eat every morning. He was with them as he provided them with the Ten Commandments so they could know how God wanted them to respond to him for all he had done out of his great love for them. Unlike the many pagans around them, who never knew exactly what they could do to placate their gods, the Israelites could now know from the Ten Commandments exactly what their God graciously wanted for the betterment of their lives.

His active presence was with them, expressed through the presence of the ark of the covenant as well as in their portable temple in the wilderness, called the tabernacle. Even the meaning of the word *tabernacle* in their language conveys the truth of God's living presence with them. Each year the people could remember with a special feast how the active presence of God was, and continued to be, with his people as they celebrated the Passover and the retelling of the liberating story of their exodus from oppression in Egypt. The very history of God's people speaks loudly and clearly about the good news of God's continued presence among them. When Christians are baptized, God is present with them through water and the word as they are united with him as his beloved children and disciples. Christians also have a special feast with roots in the Passover meal expressed in the Holy Communion, which celebrates the active and real presence of Christ with them in the bread and wine of the sacrament, forgiving them and strengthening them in their faith connection with Jesus.

When Jesus proclaimed to the people that the kingdom of heaven was "at hand," he was demonstrating the Immanuel that God himself was continuing his presence with them, even as he was throughout the Exodus experience and as they now endured the Roman oppression. He was as close to them as their very fingertips. I believe that when Jesus brought to the people the good news of the kingdom, he expressed that wonderfully essential element of the kingdom, which is experienced as the active presence of God.

SEEING THE KINGDOM METAPHORICALLY

THE BIBLE TELLS us that when Jesus spoke with people about spiritual truth, "he did not speak to them without a parable, but privately to his own disciples he explained everything" (Mark 4:34). It was easier for many people to understand difficult spiritual concepts by presenting them in the form of stories about everyday life. When Jesus spoke about the kingdom, he often used stories, parables, or metaphorical imagery.

People have always been enchanted by stories. When I was a child, I loved to listen to stories. My favorite bedtime stories were those my father often told to me. I enjoyed listening to my mother read stories to me before I could easily read them for myself. As I attended an elementary Christian day school, some of my favorite times were living with the many Bible stories. Aesop's fables and Grimm's fairy tales also stand as evidence that throughout the years stories have found a treasured and enduring place in the lives of people. Many of the stories have taught some of the underlying principles that have formed a moral compass for guiding the lives of generations.[1]

Jesus became famous for telling stories as he proclaimed the gospel of the kingdom.

A large number of the parables he told were stories specifically about the kingdom. To make his stories more understandable, the setting for his stories included events and circumstances familiar to the religious and agrarian society and culture in which he lived. Today we live in a different time, place, and culture; and those stories present us with the difficulty of discerning some of the subtleties contained in their meaning.

The parables of Jesus are stories that metaphorically proclaim a deeper spiritual meaning than what we obviously see on the surface. Jesus began a number of his kingdom parables with the words "The kingdom of heaven is like" or "The kingdom of God may be compared to," which was then be followed by a familiar earthly story. It would offer a glimpse into a deeper meaning of what the kingdom he proclaimed was like.

The number of kingdom parables Jesus told give us a clue into how important it was for him to describe the various aspects of the kingdom. Some of these stories are very familiar, while others are not so much. It was interesting for me to look again at the parables and try to discover an important principle or lesson, on which Jesus focused in the story as it pertains to the gospel of the kingdom. Let's look at a select number of parables to see what I mean.

WEEDS

Let's look at the parable of the weeds (Matt. 13:24–30, 36–43). Jesus began by saying, "The kingdom of heaven may be compared to a man who sowed good seed in his field, but while his men were sleeping, his enemy came and sowed weeds among the wheat and went away." Later, when the plants grew up, the servants asked the man whether they should pull up the weeds. Jesus said, "No, lest in gathering the weeds you root up the wheat along with them. Let both grow together until the harvest, and at harvest time I will tell the reapers, Gather the weeds first and bind them in bundles to be burned, but gather the wheat into my barn."

It is amazing that Jesus contrasted the gospel of the kingdom with an enemy of the kingdom. Here on earth it is difficult to differentiate between the good and the bad. This is like saying that it isn't possible for people to look into another person's heart so that they might make a valid judgment as to whether a person is a kingdom person or an anti-kingdom person. Great patience is what is experienced in the kingdom. Jesus said, "Let both grow together until the harvest." He reserved the pronouncement of judgment not to those still on earth but to the Son of Man at the close of the age.

THE GOOD NEWS OF THE KINGDOM

The good news is that God is extremely patient with people. The psalmist described the merciful patience of God by saying, "But you, O Lord, are a God merciful and gracious, slow to anger and abounding in steadfast love and faithfulness" (Ps. 86:15). True, there is a final determination, but until then the kingdom is mercifully nonjudgmental and patient. This isn't always the way people experience life. There are times when it seems that decisions are made without using a sufficient amount of data. So often people make judgments based solely on how they feel about a person or situation. Many decisions about people are made too quickly. We say they jump to conclusions. Other judgments are made about someone, even before there is information available about that person. Judgments based on prior, inadequate, or faulty assumptions are called "prejudgments" or "prejudices."

In this kingdom story, Jesus said that in his kingdom there is no rush to judgment on his part. People in his kingdom are cautioned to follow his example. At one point Jesus said, "Judge not, that you be not judged. For with the judgment you pronounce you will be judged, and with the measure you use it will be measured to you. Why do you see the speck that is in your brother's eye, but do not notice the log that is in your own eye? Or how can you say to your brother, 'Let me take the speck out of your eye,' when there is the log in your own eye? You hypocrite, first take the log out of your own eye, and then you will see clearly to take the speck out of your brother's eye" (Matt. 7:1–5).

In the kingdom there is to be nothing false, nor any prejudgment. Leave the judgments to God. He is a just and merciful God. For people who have been injured by prejudice or false judgment, the message of Jesus is good news. God sees everything and will finally bring to justice all that is wrong. That is what it's like to experience the gospel of the kingdom.

LEAVEN

Another kingdom story Jesus told is the parable of leaven (Luke 13:20–21). This is one of the shortest parables Jesus told, but it isn't always the easiest for people to appreciate today. He simply said, "To what shall I compare the kingdom of God? It is like leaven that a woman took and hid in three measures of flour, until it was all leavened." Leaven is also known as yeast. The Hebrew people usually understood yeast or leaven negatively. The use of leaven wasn't permitted in ritual offerings (Lev. 2:4, 11). Yeast is a certain fungus; because of its power to cause flour to rise, it is included in dough. Unleavened bread is bread made without yeast, as in making matzah. Bread made with yeast was permitted in a religious ritual only in the sacrificial bread of a peace offering for thanksgiving during the Feast of Weeks or Pentecost (Lev. 7:13–14).

Jesus used leaven in this parable as something positive rather than negative. He took something ordinarily understood as something to be eliminated as it is in certain rituals as well as in the preparation for the Passover; instead he now emphasized the powerful positive quality of the leaven to enable dough to rise.

THE GOOD NEWS OF THE KINGDOM

This positive quality of leaven is also a characteristic that is part of the kingdom. In the kingdom, what was thought of as undesirable can now be found as desirable. The kingdom, like leaven, has the powerful quality of changing what is at times thought of as undesirable to be now raised to the level of being desirable. It reminds me of the story by Hans Christian Andersen about an ugly, little duckling; after growing up, it was really a beautiful swan.

A similar concept can now be applied to people. People who were once thought of as undesirable and worthy only of being excluded can now become desirable and included in the kingdom. Gentiles, for example, were excluded from many ordinary interpersonal associations and especially prohibited from entering the temple area. Contrary to such a practice of prohibition, those who are in the kingdom are now permitted to experience a welcoming inclusion as a positive, transforming, and liberating power. That's something for which a person in the kingdom can give thanks and praise. That's a positive view of leaven, as presented in the kingdom parable of Jesus. That's good news. That's the gospel of the kingdom.

TWIN KINGDOM PARABLES

There are two kingdom parables of Jesus I call the "twin kingdom parables." These are the parable of the hidden treasure and the parable of the pearl of great value (Matt. 13:44–46). These are twin parables in the sense that they nearly speak of the same truth about the kingdom.

In the first parable Jesus said, "The kingdom of heaven is like treasure hidden in a field, which a man found and covered up. Then in his joy he goes and sells all that he has and buys that field" (Matt. 13:44). This man didn't seek out this treasure. It seems that he simply happened to come across it. In those days, there were no banks like the First Bank of Capernaum or the Bank of Galilee. Although there were people called bankers, they were much like money changers at the table. Many people who wanted to hide their accumulation of gold or silver from the tax collectors or thieves, or even from an approaching army, would bury it underground. Some of these accumulations stayed in the ground long after a person died. When this man came upon this treasure, it could perhaps be understood that the discovering of this treasure was sheer serendipity. Finding this treasure was truly an unexpected but fortuitous happening.

The man didn't expect to find the treasure, but when he did, he instantly understood that the treasure he found was something he definitely wanted. He was overjoyed at his discovery. But there was a problem. The field where he found the treasure wasn't his. He knew the treasure had great value, so he took steps to purchase the field. He sold all he had to raise enough money to buy the field and in this way come into possession of the treasure. To him selling all that he had was worth it. So he gave up all he had so he might buy the field and in this way obtain the treasure.

How is this story like the kingdom of heaven? The kingdom Jesus proclaimed wasn't always easy to see, much like the treasure hidden in a field. The kingdom remains hidden or not always obvious to everyone. This is why Jesus told stories—so that he might not only reveal the kingdom but also unearth something valuable about the kingdom.

What makes this good news? First, there really is a kingdom. To many people, it may have been hidden, but he was now making people aware of it. In addition, it was now being revealed that all people could be participants of this kingdom. It wasn't a kingdom only for the elite, the powerful, and the wealthy; it was meant for everyone. Furthermore, they would be able to count it as their most valuable treasured asset. The kingdom would be recognized as being so valuable to them that they would be willing to sacrifice everything for the sake of the kingdom.

The second of the twin parables is the story of a man in search of a pearl of great value. Jesus said, "Again, the kingdom of heaven is like a merchant in search of fine pearls. Who, on finding one pearl of great value, went and sold all that he had and bought it" (Matt. 13:45–46). In this story the pearl that was very valuable is much like the treasure hidden in a field. In both stories what was considered valuable and desirable ended up being like the kingdom. In one story the treasure wasn't something consciously sought, but in the other story the valuable pearl was sought after with intentionality. In both stories the men were willing to give up all they had to make their discovery their own.

THE GOOD NEWS OF THE KINGDOM

The good news of the kingdom is that it is recognized as so desirable that when a person finds it, it is worth giving up anything else to make it one's own. The good news of the kingdom is that when a person seeks after something to enrich one's life, it is the kingdom that makes life so completely fulfilling that there is no need to continue to search for more or cling to anything else. Finally obtaining what one spends his or her life pursuing isn't always what happens. At times a person is finally disappointed in securing what took so much time and energy to obtain.

Such a pursuit reminds me of a man in the desert who, in the heat of the sun, is thirsting to death and is desperately trudging forward toward a lake of water, which unfortunately turns out to be nothing more than a mirage. The kingdom Jesus proclaims is no mirage. The kingdom of God is real, good, and appropriate for a life pursuit. It is good to remember that Jesus said, "But seek first the kingdom of God and his righteousness, and all these things will be added to you" (Matt. 6:33).

A treasure or valuable pearl amounts to nothing compared to the value of being a citizen of the kingdom Jesus proclaimed. If anything is to be sought in life, it is to be intimately connected with Jesus and his kingdom.

The Net

Jesus told a kingdom story about a fisherman's net (Matt. 13:47–50). "Again, the kingdom of heaven is like a net that was thrown into the sea and gathered fish of every kind. When it was full, men drew it ashore and sat down and sorted the good into containers but threw away the bad. So it will be at the close of the age. The angels will come out and separate the evil from the righteous and throw them into the fiery furnace. In that place there will be weeping and gnashing of teeth."

This parable of Jesus shows that the kingdom includes not only the present or workaday lives of people, but it also concerns itself with the end of time, which Jesus called "the close of the age." The net tells us that the kingdom is open for everyone. You don't have to be recommended by someone, pass a test, or meet any other kind of requirement. During this lifetime, no prejudgment is made. The net is open for all.

The judgment, Jesus said, comes at the close of the age. He pictured the judgment as being done by the angels. The evil is separated from the righteous, since the good fish are separated from whatever else was caught in the net. My father had a net. It was a small net, which we called a "seine." The seine was used to catch minnows used as live bait for fishing.

One day the pastor's son wanted to go fishing and decided to go out and seine for minnows. He asked to borrow daddy's seine. He also took me along to hold the other end of the net. We went to a creek that is locally known as Uncle John's Creek to catch the minnows. We walked through the shallow water with the net and then took it to the bank of the creek to take the minnows out of the net. It was at this point that I discovered we had caught not only a number of minnows; also in the net were these dark, little creatures. They were not only in the net, but a few had fastened themselves onto our legs. They were leeches!

We not only quickly pulled these blood suckers off our legs and also promptly disposed of them as we also did with the leeches still caught in the net. The minnows were saved and placed in a minnow bucket to keep them alive. In the parable, Jesus told us that everything in the net that wasn't a good fish he called evil, and they are thrown into a fiery furnace where there would be weeping and gnashing of teeth. During this lifetime, anyone who claims to be, or pretends to be, in the kingdom is permitted, but the final determination as to who remains and who doesn't is decided at the close of the age.

The Good News of the Kingdom

This parable sounds rather severe. Where is the good news in it? We need to remember that, as we live in the present kingdoms of this world, we can experience oppression of all kinds. Jesus once said, "In the world you will have tribulation. But take heart; I have overcome the world" (John 16:33). The early Christians who were experiencing difficulty were told by the apostle, "Through many tribulations we must enter the kingdom of God" (Acts 14:22). The kingdom Jesus proclaimed is a kingdom that offers hope.

Even in this world, the righteous experience difficulty, but at the close of the age, the evil will be separated from the righteous. Evil will be cast out. The kingdom Jesus proclaimed is a kingdom where the trouble experienced in this world's kingdoms cannot only be endured but will finally come to an end. Evil will be cast out. There will be an absence of tribulation at the close of the age. There will be an end to evil, and the righteous will be saved. Must we always wait until the end of the age? No, Jesus is with us to strengthen us during difficult times, and with him there is always victory and hope, even during times of stress and hardship. That's the good news of the kingdom.

The Unforgiving Servant

Jesus told a story that has come to be known as either the unmerciful servant or the unforgiving servant (Matt. 18:23–34). Either name fits as a meaningful title for this parable. For some reason Jesus felt that this story would help to explain what the gospel of the kingdom is like. Read it for yourself and see.

> Therefore the kingdom of heaven may be compared to a king who wished to settle accounts with his servants. When he began to settle, one was brought to him who owed him ten thousand talents. And since he could not pay, his master ordered him to be sold, with his wife and children and all that he had, and payment to be made. So the servant fell on his knees, imploring him, "Have patience with me, and I will pay you everything." And out of pity for him, the master of that servant released him and forgave him the debt. But when that same servant went out, he found one of his fellow servants who owed him a hundred denarii, and seizing him, he began to choke him, saying, "Pay what you owe." So his fellow servant fell down and pleaded with him, "Have patience with me, and I will pay you."

He refused and went and put him in prison until he should pay the debt. When his fellow servants saw what had taken place, they were greatly distressed, and they went and reported to their master all that had taken place. Then his master summoned him and said to him. "You wicked servant! I forgave you all that debt because you pleaded with me. And should not you have had mercy on your fellow servant, as I had mercy on you?" And in anger his master delivered him to the jailers, until he should pay all his debt. So also my heavenly Father will do to every one of you, if you do not forgive your brother from your heart.

How much debt is too much debt? Obviously, too much debt is an amount that is so great that repaying it would be impossible. This is exactly the predicament the servant was in when he was first brought before the king. The parable describes it this way: "He could not pay." The amount mentioned in the story is "ten thousand talents," or, simply stated, it was more than any one person who was a servant could accumulate during a lifetime.

Many people today owe money on their houses, cars, credit cards, medical costs, and a great many other debts. It all amounts to an enormous amount of money. There may be some who owe so much debt that it couldn't be eliminated in a lifetime. Some may think of the trillions of dollars of debt the United States owes and wonder whether it can ever be eradicated.

As the servant fell to his knees, clearly he understood his impossible predicament and could do nothing else but beg the king for patience and mercy. At this point in the story, we are shown the loving-kindness and generosity of heart the king possessed. The king wasn't required to show any leniency to the servant. The money owed to the king was his own money. This was a legitimate debt. There was no evidence presented that indicates the servant deserved to receive any compassionate consideration whatsoever. If the king would show any kindness, it would be a kindness shown to an undeserving person. The king did this. He graciously forgave the servant of all his debt.

Jesus now turned his attention back to the forgiven servant. Freed from his debt, the servant went to his fellow servant who owed him a smaller amount of debt. "He began to choke him, saying, 'Pay what you owe.'" When his fellow servant pled for mercy, he refused and instead had his fellow servant thrown into prison. The king heard of how his servant, whom he had forgiven all his debt, had treated his fellow servant. "Then his master summoned him and said to him, 'You wicked servant! I forgave you all that debt because you pleaded with me. And should not you have had mercy on your fellow servant, as I had mercy on you?'"

Jesus told this story as an answer to Peter, who immediately asked prior to the parable, "'Lord, how often will my brother sin against me, and I forgive him? As many as seven times?' Jesus said to him, 'I do not say to you seven times, but seventy times seven'" (Matt. 18:21–22).

Jesus's answer indicates that a person should forgive not just once or even several times but repeatedly. This isn't what the wicked servant did. Jesus taught this lesson on forgiveness when he taught the disciples to pray the Lord's Prayer and then followed the prayer with these words. "For if you forgive men when they sin against you, your heavenly Father will also forgive you. But if you do not forgive men their sin, your Father will not forgive your sins" (Matt. 6:14–15).

The Good News of the Kingdom

The good news of the kingdom Jesus showed to us in this parable is that in the kingdom there is forgiveness. The king forgives. At the same time, we are taught to be responsive to the forgiving grace the King of the kingdom showed us. That's what the kingdom is about. When such a gracious responsiveness of forgiveness is in turn given to those who have sinned against us, we live in the happy spirit of the gospel of the kingdom.

Why is it so important to forgive those who sin against us? The answer is that it's actually in our own best interest to forgive others. Living with an unforgiving attitude or spirit is often explained by recognizing that refusing to forgive is like holding on to a corrosive acid. Refusing to forgive hurts the person who won't forgive more than it does the one who sinned against him or her. The good news of the kingdom tells us that just as our King Jesus forgives us, so also we can now have the power to respond and graciously forgive those who sin against us.

The Needle's Eye

There is a saying of Jesus that might cause a person to think twice about who can enter the kingdom of heaven. Jesus said, "'Truly, I say to you, only with difficulty will a rich person enter the kingdom of heaven. Again I tell you, it is easier for a camel to go through the eye of a needle than for a rich person to enter the kingdom of God.' When the disciples heard this, they were greatly astonished, saying,

'Who then can be saved?' But Jesus looked at them and said, 'With man this is impossible, but with God all things are possible'" (Matt. 19:23–26).

Entrance into the kingdom is available to everyone. This was made clear when Jesus told the story about the fishing net, which is open to gather all kinds of fish. In this saying about a camel and the eye of a needle, Jesus cautioned that there is something that makes it extremely difficult to enter the kingdom. He used this metaphorical expression, which says it is easier for a very large animal, a camel, to pass through a very small opening, the eye of a needle, than it is for a rich person to enter the kingdom of God.

People who have dogs as pets sometimes make a small doggie door, through which their dog can easily go in and out of the house. I know of a family whose pet died, and they later got another dog. The problem was, this new dog was bigger than their last dog, and this dog was too big to squeeze through the little doggie door. Their doggie door had to be made bigger. This situation and the example Jesus made of the camel and the eye of a needle remind me of another saying of Jesus. "For the gate is narrow and the way is hard that leads to life, and those who find it are few" (Matt. 7:14). We must take care that we don't become too big in respect to our attachment to worldly goods and arrogant pride that we cannot enter the kingdom.

Some say that the needle's eye actually refers to a small gate that exists within a larger gate of an ancient city. The smaller gate within the larger gate would permit a person to enter without opening the very much larger gate. I recall that when I was in Jerusalem, there was such an arrangement at the Jaffa Gate. The smaller gate is referred to as the "needle's eye." A large camel couldn't pass through this smaller gate except perhaps by removing all the baggage the camel was carrying and getting it down on its knees; then with great difficulty it could crawl through the needle's eye to enter the city.

A rich man's riches may be like the baggage the camel carried. Kneeling down to crawl through the needle's eye may be likened to a rich man giving up the pride of his self-made accomplishments to reach his rich status and admitting he was truly a humble person.

In the original language of the Bible, the word for camel is only one letter different from the word used for a large rope. When one speaks the word, it even sounds very much like the word used for the word *camel*. Perhaps Jesus actually said, "It is easier for a rope to go through the eye of a needle than for a rich person to enter the kingdom of God." Even if Jesus did say *rope* instead of *camel*, the meaning of his saying would be the same. I think I will stay with the regular needle and camel instead of the needle and rope. The camel with the eye of the needle is also much more picturesque and clarifying language.

The meaning of this kingdom saying of Jesus is simply that one's accomplishments, no matter how great they appear, are not great enough to gain entrance into the kingdom. It's like Jesus said, "Only with difficulty will a rich person enter the kingdom of heaven." The disciples responded to this saying of Jesus with the question "Who then can be saved?" Jesus said, "With man this is impossible, but with God all things are possible (Matt. 19:26)." A person cannot enter the kingdom by paying for it with riches or by using his or her great accomplishments. Entrance into the kingdom is by God's grace alone, not by trusting in one's own riches or efforts.

THE GOOD NEWS OF THE KINGDOM

The bad news would be if a person is rich or has led an exemplary life with many good deeds to one's credit; the bad news would be if such a person would be given preference with respect to entering the kingdom. Such a policy would cause me to wonder whether I was rich enough or had done enough good deeds to be granted entrance into the kingdom. Such a policy wouldn't make me feel very confident about my prospects of being acceptable to God. I would have no certainty about living with any kind of peace with God.

The good news is that Jesus proclaimed that trusting in riches or good deeds will in fact make it extremely difficult, if not impossible, to enter the kingdom. People of the kingdom will do good things and use their God-given talents to increase their wealth. They will do so not to gain any preferences but to be loving and helpful to others, and to show their appreciation and gratitude to God for his love, grace, and mercy shown to them.

THE GENEROUS MASTER

I'm not aware of any labor unions at the time of Jesus. If there had been, I doubt the kingdom story Jesus told about the laborers in the vineyard (Matt. 20:1–16) would have been told in the same way it appears in the Bible. Jesus said,

> For the kingdom of heaven is like a master of a
> house who went out early in the morning to hire
> laborers for his vineyard. After agreeing with the
> laborers for a denarius a day, he sent them into his

vineyard. And going out about the third hour he saw others standing idle in the marketplace, and to them he said, "You go into the vineyard too, and whatever is right I will give you." So they went. Going out again about the sixth hour and the ninth hour, he did the same. And about the eleventh hour he went out and found others standing. And he said to them, "Why do you stand here idle all day?" They said to him, "Because no one has hired us." He said to them, "You go into the vineyard too." And when evening came, the owner of the vineyard said to his foreman, "Call the laborers and pay them their wages, beginning with the last, up to the first." And when those hired about the eleventh hour came, each of them received a denarius. Now when those hired first came, they thought they would receive more, but each of them also received a denarius. And on receiving it they grumbled at the master of the house, saying, "These last worked only one hour, and you have made them equal to us who have borne the burden of the day and the scorching heat." But he replied to one of them, "Friend, I am doing you no wrong. Did you not agree with me for a denarius? Take what belongs to you and go. I choose to give to this last worker as I give to you. Am I not allowed to do what I choose with what belongs to me? Or do you begrudge my generosity?" So the last will be first, and the first last.

What Jesus depicted to us in this story about the kingdom is the difference between this world's values and the values in the gospel of the kingdom. This is the point the story makes by using wages and time worked as the world's criteria of what makes one worthy of being in God's kingdom. A person who works the hardest and longest under severe conditions should be recognized as more worthy and valued more highly for inclusion in the kingdom than one whose work is easier, under the best of conditions, and who works less time. Jesus, on the other hand, seemed to be saying that the master's decision concerning wages illustrates that in the kingdom of heaven there are no differences made in respect to any person. The difference rests with the master. He extends his grace to all; that is, anything a person receives is received because of the generosity of the master alone.

When evaluating this decision of the master in comparison to this world's values, it is easy to see that some of the workers in the vineyard became upset. Whether they were upset over what they viewed as being unfair or that they reacted with envy isn't said, but it is revealed that they "grumbled at the master of the house." The workers recognized differences, whereas the master recognized no differences. He responded to their complaints saying, "Friend, I am doing you no wrong. Did you not agree with me for a denarius? Take what belongs to you and go. I choose to give to the last worker as I give to you. Am I not allowed to do what I choose with what belongs to me? Or do you begrudge my generosity?"

THE GOOD NEWS OF THE KINGDOM

The gospel of the kingdom doesn't view the worthiness or unworthiness of people according to this world's standards, which aren't always God's standards. There are times when something may be legally right but morally wrong. There may be times when our human reason seems right while God's understanding is different.

One time the apostles were arrested for teaching people about Jesus. When they were told to stop, Peter answered, "We must obey God rather than men" (Acts 5:29). The standards of men aren't always the standards of God. When Jesus explained the reason for his unexpected pay scale, he described this upside-down standard of the kingdom as "So the last will be first, and the first last." Grace, not this world's standards, becomes the basis for a person's worthiness in the kingdom Jesus proclaimed. In his kingdom all are offered the same based not on any ranking or on what a person does or doesn't do, but it is solely based on the loving-kindness and grace of God. We have no reason to begrudge his treatment of us. For his kind of treatment to all undeserving people, we can only be thankful and rejoice. That's the gospel of the kingdom.

THE RIGHT GARMENT

Jesus once told a story in the presence of some of the temple establishment about a wedding feast to illustrate something about those admitted to the kingdom. He said,

> The kingdom of heaven may be compared to a king who gave a wedding feast for his son, and sent his servants to call those who were invited to the wedding feast, but they would not come. Again he sent other servants, saying, "Tell those who are invited, See, I have prepared my dinner, my oxen and my fat calves have been slaughtered, and everything is ready. Come to the wedding feast." But they paid no attention and went off, one to his farm, another to his business, while the rest seized his servants, treated them shamefully, and killed them. The king

was angry, and he sent his troops and destroyed those murderers and burned their city. Then he said to his servants, "The wedding feast is ready, but those invited were not worthy. Go therefore to the main roads and invite to the wedding feast as many as you find." And those servants went out into the roads and gathered all whom they found, both bad and good. So the wedding hall was filled with guests.

But when the king came in to look at the guests, he saw there a man who had no wedding garment. And he said to him, "Friend, how did you get in here without a wedding garment?" And he was speechless. Then the king said to the attendants, "Bind him hand and foot and cast him into the outer darkness. In that place there will be weeping and gnashing of teeth." For many are called, but few are chosen. (Matt. 22:2–14)

The chief priests and Pharisees who heard this parable were accustomed to thinking that only those acceptable to God were those who were like them while all others were excluded. The story of Jesus destroys that kind of exclusivity. The king's servants "went out into the roads and gathered all whom they found, both bad and good. So the wedding hall was filled with guests."

In the Middle East and even in Rome, the host was accustomed to furnishing wedding garments to all who were invited. This detail reminds me of what Isaiah 61:10 mentions. "I will greatly rejoice in the Lord; my soul shall exult in my God, for he has clothed me with the garments of salvation; he has covered me with the robe of righteousness, as a bridegroom decks himself like a priest with a beautiful headdress, and as a bride adorns herself with her jewels."

In the story Jesus said that all who were at the wedding feast wore wedding garments except one, who evidently thought wearing his own clothing was suitable enough, perhaps even superior. The king noticed and had him thrown out. It seems likely that Jesus indicated that this person, like so many chief priests and Pharisees at that time, thought his own goodness, which he evidently considered much better than that of the others, was good enough or even preferable for him to be included. Obviously, he was mistaken.

Jesus concluded his story with the expression "For many are called, but few are chosen." Many receive God's invitation to receive a garment of righteousness, which qualifies them for inclusion in his kingdom. Some refuse God's invitation for his garment of righteousness when they think their own garment of goodness qualifies them for inclusion in his kingdom.

The Good News of the Kingdom

It's no secret that some youngsters have tried to use falsified or counterfeit identifications to enter an establishment intended only for adults. Or perhaps you have received an invitation to a black-tie event. If you had attended such an event in a T shirt, blue jeans, and flip-flops, there is a good possibility that you might have been summarily ostracized. In the kingdom story Jesus told, he included not only a gracious invitation to a grand wedding feast but also a solemn warning.

What is the gospel, the good news, of the kingdom? It's that King Jesus offers his robe of righteousness, which is available for all who accept it. If you refuse the garment the King furnishes and try to wear your own garment, perhaps thinking your own garment of righteousness is good enough or even better than the one the King furnishes, your exclusion will be imminent.

The wedding feast is a literary picture of the kingdom. The garment represents one's acceptability or worthiness for being part of the kingdom. The garment given to those in his kingdom is one of righteousness. Righteousness is the requirement for entrance into the kingdom. One's own righteousness isn't good enough. Everyone needs to be clothed in the perfect righteousness of King Jesus himself. This righteousness is graciously and freely given to all who would receive it. It's a good thing to recognize that our own goodness and righteousness aren't good enough and must be discarded and then in faith receive the righteousness of Jesus. This reminds me of a very old hymn by Ludwig von Zinzendorf and translated by John Wesley.

> Jesus, Thy blood and righteousness
> My beauty are, my glorious dress;
> Midst flaming world, in these arrayed,
> With joy shall I lift up my head.[2]

Ten Virgins

Jesus used his kingdom stories to give people insights into what the kingdom was all about. No parabolic stories of his revealed everything about the kingdom, but they did provide windows through which we can get a glimpse of what he meant. The stories Jesus told provided not only insight but also hope, encouragement, and even warnings in respect to the kingdom.

Consider the kingdom story Jesus told about time limitations in respect to entering the kingdom. The story written in Matthew 25:1–13 has been traditionally known as the parable of the ten virgins. Jesus said,

> Then the kingdom of heaven will be like ten virgins who took their lamps and went to meet the bridegroom. Five of them were foolish, and five were wise. For when the foolish took their lamps, they took no oil with them, but the wise took flasks of oil with their lamps. As the bridegroom was delayed, they all became drowsy and slept. But at midnight there was a cry, "Here is the bridegroom! Come out to meet him." Then all those virgins rose and trimmed their lamps. And the foolish said to the wise, "Give us some of your oil, for our lamps are going out." But the wise answered, saying, "Since there will not be enough for us and for you, go rather to the dealers and buy for yourselves." And while they were going to buy, the bridegroom came, and those who were ready went in with him to the marriage feast, and the door was shut. Afterward the other virgins came also, saying, Lord, lord, open to us." But he answered, "Truly, I say to you, I do not know you." Watch therefore, for you know neither the day nor the hour.

There seems to be a deadline for almost everything. A ticket for a concert, a coupon for a supermarket item, or an airline ticket are only a few items that have limitations concerning the time when they expire. The same is true in the story Jesus told about the ten virgins regarding the timing in gaining entrance into the bridegroom's wedding feast.

The five wise virgins entered the wedding feast when the bridegroom arrived because they were on time, arriving before the deadline and being well prepared to meet him. The five foolish virgins came late, missing the deadline, because they weren't well prepared to meet him, and they weren't admitted to the bridegroom's wedding feast.

In this kingdom story Jesus is traditionally understood as the bridegroom. He will come at the end of time for those well prepared to meet him when he arrives. At that point they will be received into the everlasting wedding feast; that is, they will be welcomed into his timeless kingdom forever. Those who aren't ready won't gain entrance into the complete fullness of his everlasting kingdom.

What is it that makes us well prepared to meet God at the end of time? In the parable, what made them ready to meet the bridegroom was oil in their lighted lamps. If the lamp can be thought of as a person's life, he or she has the one ingredient that enables that life to be alive with light. This is someone whose inner faith connection with God is the oil that enables one's life to shine with the life light, which can endure forever. Without that inner faith and trust connection with God, a person's life won't have the energy needed to live forever.

THE GOOD NEWS OF THE KINGDOM

There will finally come a time at the end of the age when the kingdom Jesus proclaimed will come into its glorious, everlasting fullness. Now during our lifetimes everyone needs to be aware that there are preparedness and time limitations. We don't know when the end of time will happen. We must always be prepared to meet Jesus at the Lord's final arrival. On a more personal level, we don't know the time of our own end of life. Whether we are speaking of the end of time itself or the end of our own lifetimes, the same thing will take place; the bridegroom Jesus will arrive for us. Will we be prepared to meet Jesus at the appointed time and so enter the everlasting kingdom?

A popular saying is true that prior planning pays. Most of my life I've lived either in what is called "Tornado Alley" or in the greater New Orleans area, where hurricanes occur. It's best to always have an emergency supply of food and water, a flashlight, a battery-operated or oil lamp available in the event the winds come and the electrical system fails. If you don't prepare ahead of time, you will very likely end up hungry, thirsty, and in the dark. In much the same way, it is time that we examine the condition of our own faith to ensure our own readiness to meet the bridegroom. The good news of the kingdom is that we can be prepared with the inner light of faith that connects us with Jesus. A person who is alive with the light of faith will be ready and welcome to enter the final wedding feast of Jesus, the bridegroom, the complete fullness of the everlasting kingdom. That is the good news of the kingdom Jesus proclaimed.

The Mystery of the Seed

Again, Jesus told a kingdom story of the growing seed. "The kingdom of God is as if a man should scatter seed on the ground. He sleeps and rises night and day, and the seed sprouts and grows; he knows not how. The earth produces by itself, first the blade, then the ear, then the full grain in the ear. But when the grain is ripe, at once he puts in the sickle, because the harvest has come" (Mark 4:26–29).

THE GOOD NEWS OF THE KINGDOM

The good news is that we can finally admit that there is mystery regarding the kingdom. It's a good mystery. We don't know everything there is to know about how the kingdom works. Christians have been accused of hiding behind the concept of mystery. Whenever anything in the Bible cannot be rationally explained to the satisfaction of those who can be satisfied only with a scientific explanation, it is said that believers in the Bible simply called it a "mystery" and in this way avoided admitting the Bible is unscientific and has little place in our present world.

Believers, on the other hand, often wonder why the scientific community cannot also honestly admit that there is much mystery that also interjects itself into what is known and unknown in the scientific investigation of the natural world. Surprise! Science cannot answer everything. Surprise again! The Bible doesn't answer all scientific questions. This is actually a non-argument. Christians are also part of the scientific community in pursuit of answers about how the earth and the universe work. Mystery is actually not a negative but an incentive for both scientists and biblical scholars to search for a wider, deeper understanding and clearer truth.

The farmer who sows the seed in the ground knows he is working only on the surface. He may know the conditions needed for seeds to grow, but he must rely on that mystery he cannot control, which actually gives the seed the power to sprout and grow. Does that mystery prevent the farmer from farming? Of course not. Does the mystery of the kingdom negate the existence of the kingdom? Of course not. What does the mystery tell us? It says us that the kingdom exists and works, even though we're unable to understand or control everything about it. The kingdom exists and works because of the gracious power and working of the king. What good is there for us in this mystery? It's comforting to know that there is no absolute necessity to understand every detail about how the kingdom works. God, the King, is in control. This fact enables us to live and work confidently, joyfully, and full of faith and trust within the mystery of the kingdom. That's the good news of the kingdom Jesus proclaimed.

Can You See the Bird's Nest?

This is one of my favorite kingdom stories Jesus told. He said, "The kingdom of heaven is like a grain of mustard seed that a man took and sowed in his field. It is the smallest of all seeds, but when it has grown it is larger than all the garden plants and becomes a tree, so that the birds of the air come and make nests in its branches" (Matt. 13:31–32).

Can you see the bird's nest in my mustard tree? Can you see what the good news of the kingdom is like in this simple kingdom story Jesus told? I believe Jesus tells this and other stories to transport our minds into a realm that goes beyond what we ordinarily see.

What goes beyond what we normally see? Let me share with you how my artist wife, Betty, helped me to see beyond what most people think we see.

We were in a park in the city of New Orleans. She said, "What do you see?"

I said, "Trees with branches and leaves."

"Oh, my," she responded, "and what color are the trees and leaves?"

I said, "Well, the tree and branches are brown, and the leaves are green."

She laughed. I felt a little silly. Why did she laugh? She saw so much more than I did. She said, "No, no, no, the trees in the shady areas are purple, and the leaves are all different colors and shades of greens and yellows and blue."

Even when she tried to explain, it was difficult for me to see purple trees. My eyes hadn't yet been opened to see what an artist might see or to understand what she meant by "purple."

Coincidently, as I'm writing this, a report is being made on television. It is being reported that with new instrumentation astronomers can now better detect or *see* dark matter in the universe, which previously couldn't be seen. It seems to me that this may be similar to what some people may have experienced when Jesus told his parables. Not everyone could see the truths brought out in the parables. Spiritual truths were spoken of using earthly examples, which may give a glimpse into the spiritual truth, but those truths evidently couldn't be totally revealed using earthly examples in human language. Sometimes even his closest disciples, who heard Jesus for several years, needed further amplification or explanations of his stories. Can you see the bird's nest in my mustard tree?

Some of the studies I did while working toward a doctorate took place in the Holy Land. One day we were in Bethany to visit the tomb of Lazarus. As in most biblically historical sites, churches have been built at these places to protect and remember that site. So it is with the tomb of Lazarus. We entered what might be understood as the basement of the church. It is there that we saw what is thought to be the original entrance to the tomb. The entrance to the tomb seen outside the church was added later. As we proceeded outside the church to this traditional entrance, there happened to be at that time a large mustard plant growing along the side of the church. This mustard plant was large enough to be called a tree. Mustard plants often grew wild in the farmer's field. They were often considered a nuisance and were destroyed before they grew very tall. This particular mustard plant growing near the outer entrance to Lazarus's tomb was taller than I am, and I am only about two inches shorter than six feet. This mustard tree could easily have supported a bird's nest. The parable Jesus told about the mustard seed growing into a tree and containing a bird's nest can be understood as being literally true. Jesus evidently made the point that the kingdom of God on earth may have small or humble beginnings, such as the tiny mustard seed, but it would mightily expand to the extent that the mustard plant would grow so big that it could be called a tree large enough to support a bird's nest.

But wait! People may often hear about the tiny mustard seed and how it grows into a very large plant, a plant that becomes so large Jesus even referred to it as a tree. How often do those same people, when hearing this story, stop to contemplate the bird's nest? It is almost as if the poor bird's nest gets ignored. Our attention can become so transfixed on the mustard tree—it is bigger after all— that we don't seem to see the little bird's nest. Many people have read the parable, but the bird's nest made no impression on them. True, the bird's nest in Jesus's story indicates an obvious contrast of smaller to the greater. The tiny mustard seed grew so big that it became like a tree that could even support a bird's nest. Can you see the bird's nest in the mustard tree? This may be one reason why the gospel of the kingdom seems so mysterious to us. Our attention has been diverted somehow from the gospel of the kingdom, which Jesus proclaimed, and has become focused on other things, as important as they may be. The mustard tree and the bird's nest are actually a unit, and our eyes must be able to see this unit of tree and nest as an example, a metaphor of the kingdom.

As in all the parables Jesus told, there may be one overall intended meaning for each parable, but there various additional insights can also be discerned. For example, bird's nests in mustard trees are not where birds live but where baby birds are hatched. It is from their beginnings in the nest that the birds are then launched to grow up and fulfill their destiny. Once again we see the contrast between the smaller and the larger. A small egg comes first; then a tiny bird finally grows large enough to fly out of the nest. So it is with the kingdom on earth. The kingdom grows from its smallest origins and is then launched to fulfill its greater mission.

Another explanation of the birds that have nests in the tree is that this has a reference to the Romans. This kind of association is like the one that at times is done with the figure of speech Jesus used when he said, "Foxes have holes, and birds of the air have nests, but the Son of Man has nowhere to lay his head" (Luke 9:58). The foxes are identified as those who were with Herod (Luke 13:32), and the birds are also identified as Romans with their eagle standard. When we use this kind of association for the bird's nest in the mustard tree, the identification could certainly include the Gentile world; that is, the kingdom should be seen as offering a place for those outside the Hebrew or Jewish world.[3] Although the kingdom story of Jesus doesn't explicitly mention that the pagan world is what Jesus meant by the inclusion of the bird's nest, it is certainly congruent with the overall scriptural message concerning the extension of the kingdom into the Gentile world.

Birds can also be seen as representative of the freedom the gospel of the kingdom offers because there is no confinement to the nest or the tree, but there is freedom in their flight from the nest. This understanding can be seen as a reference to those born into the Hebrew faith or heritage but who are now given the freedom of the gospel in the kingdom. At the same time, we must be aware that there is the danger of going beyond the original point of comparison when trying to understand a parable. A fertile imagination can reach some rather fanciful conclusions in attempts to gain some insight in every detail.

This may be one reason why the gospel of the kingdom seems so mysterious to us. Our attention can be diverted somehow from the gospel of the kingdom Jesus proclaimed and can become focused on other things, as interesting as they may be. The mustard tree and the bird's nest are a unit, and our eyes must be able to see this unit of tree and nest as an example, a metaphor of the kingdom. When we ask whether you can see the bird's nest in my mustard tree, we are simply asking whether we can see the gospel of the kingdom Jesus was really proclaiming. Asking this question is also asking whether we can see an underlying truth, which on the surface can for some be easily overlooked.

At the same time, the metaphor of the bird's nest and the mustard tree must point us to something very important about the gospel of the kingdom. The mustard seed is pointed out as being one of the very smallest of seeds. The mustard tree is presented as a very large tree that is so large that it can support a bird's nest. There is an obvious contrast Jesus was making here. This also corresponds to a contrast about the kingdom, which at that time was often wrongly thought to be a political-military kind of kingdom as opposed to the gospel of the kingdom, which Jesus was actually proclaiming.

The disciples themselves, who had followed Jesus closely for a number of years, still had difficulty discerning the basic understanding of the gospel of the kingdom Jesus proclaimed. Their misunderstanding is betrayed by their striking question to Jesus just before his ascension. They asked him, "Lord will you at this time restore the kingdom to Israel?" (Acts 1:6). This is an obvious reference to an earthly restoration of a kingdom like the one David and Solomon ruled. This is the kind of kingdom Jesus refuted when he told Pontius Pilate, "My kingdom is not of this world. If my kingdom were of this world, my servants would have been fighting, that I might not be delivered over to the Jews. But my kingdom is not from the world" (John 18:36). The contrast of the two kinds of kingdoms is portrayed in the contrast made in the parable of the mustard seed and mustard tree. The kingdom Jesus was speaking about in this parable isn't a reference to a military-political entity but to the king's domain, which is often not seen but is nevertheless real, alive, and expansive.

THE GOOD NEWS OF THE KINGDOM

The idea of contrast made in the parable teaches us that in the kingdom there is a contrast between what is materially easily seen and what exists but cannot be so easily and directly seen in our three-dimensional world. There is a contrast between what is perceived as very small or even insignificant that is in reality very great and quite significant. What was wrongly expected is actually something that is newer and greater than the expected. A seed that on the surface shows no sign of life becomes something alive and growing. Out of death comes life. Out of disappointment comes hope. The plant that was often thought of as worthless and undesirable becomes something desirable and of great worth. What may be seen as having no potential becomes full of potential. What couldn't be seen suddenly becomes experiential. That's the good news of the kingdom Jesus proclaimed. Can you see the bird's nest in my mustard tree?

THE KINGDOM IS
MULTIDIMENSIONAL

JESUS SPOKE OF the kingdom as being as real and as present as he himself was real and present among the people. Yet he said, "The kingdom of God is not coming with signs to be observed, nor will they say, 'Look, here it is!' or 'There!'" (Luke 17:20–21). The kingdom is beyond a location that can be pinpointed by a global positioning system. When Jesus taught his disciples to pray, he said, "Your kingdom come, your will be done, on earth as it is in heaven" (Matt. 6:10). The kingdom can be on earth, and it can be in heaven. Heaven and earth are understood to be two different realms or two different dimensions, yet the kingdom can evidently exist in those two dimensions simultaneously; that is, the kingdom in heaven doesn't cease to exist when the kingdom is experienced here on earth. The kingdom on earth doesn't cease to exist when it is experienced in heaven.

When we speak of the kingdom regarding time, we can speak of it as being real not only in the past but extending within the present and into the future. In the Lord's Prayer, Jesus said, "Your kingdom come." This indicates that the kingdom isn't always a kingdom that is an expressed reality within the realm of time on earth, but Jesus taught us to pray that it might become an expressed reality on earth just as it is always a present reality in the heavenly realm. As that prayer is answered, it is evident that the kingdom together with its blessings in the heavenly realm can also be an expected reality within the realm of time, space, and matter here on earth. In the prayer, we then continue to pray that the kingdom will come among us as an expressed reality among us. When I pray this petition, I think of it as a prayer to extend the blessings of the kingdom among those who haven't yet received it into their lives. As such, it becomes a mission prayer for the extension of the kingdom with its blessings into the lives of those who aren't yet within the kingdom. As this prayer is answered, the kingdom extends its influence, then within the lives of those in our earthly realm of time, space, and matter.

When we speak of the kingdom as being in heaven, we identify it as existing in a timeless or eternal dimension. How can this be explained? When the Christian church summarized its faith in the ecumenical creeds, it spoke of "the communion of saints." The saints who are the believers here on earth are united in a community of their faith with one another and with the saints in heaven. The saints on earth and the saints already fully experiencing the heavenly realm of the kingdom actually have a communion or real connection with one another. There is a nexus that exists between the earthly and heavenly dimensions—between the realm of timelessness and our realm of time, space, and matter. The theologian Paul Tillich once said, "Infinity is not a realm beyond the finite but rather includes the finite within itself."[1] The kingdom is multidimensional.

Clearly it was difficult for the people during the earthly ministry of Jesus to grasp the meaning of what the kingdom was. This is evident from the fact that Jesus used a number of different parables to help describe it. It is also difficult for us to comprehend what the kingdom is today. Can you see the bird's nest in my mustard tree? When Jesus proclaimed the gospel of the kingdom, he was not only saying that no matter how terrible the present situation is, we can all look forward to a better hereafter. He wasn't simply saying that the kingdom is just something spiritual. If we relegate the kingdom as simply something spiritual, we run the risk of almost placing it in a dubious "once upon a time" realm of fantasy or of "pie in the sky."

In his descriptions of the kingdom, Jesus presented a kingdom reality that can actually be experienced in the here and now. Although he also spoke of a kingdom that can be experienced within oneself, he didn't restrict the kingdom to a subjective feeling that has no objective reality. The gospel of the kingdom can be experienced in our earthly lives as an objective reality, yet it is also simultaneously beyond what we ordinarily understand as an earthly reality. When Jesus told the parable of the mustard seed, it helped me more clearly perceive what Jesus was revealing concerning the kingdom. The gospel of the kingdom is something lively, growing, purposeful in the present, and also simultaneously something one is able to express as experiencing it in its completion in the realm of timelessness.

The kingdom is multidimensional. It is mysterious because it is large and multidimensional, and yet at the same time it is so intimately involved in the very smallest facets of our lives. It is within us, and it is objectively outside and beyond us.

THE GOOD NEWS OF THE KINGDOM

As people who follow Jesus, we have much to experience in his kingdom now, and we can continue to look forward to his fully revealed kingdom after this life. That's not all. We are also given the privilege of sharing the proclamation of the gospel of the kingdom with those who haven't known Jesus or the good news of his kingdom. People who come to know Jesus and follow him are sometimes called "disciples of Jesus." A disciple is someone who, having come to know Jesus and trusted him to be his or her savior and king, is now one who has become a disciplined follower of him—that is, a disciple. When we share Jesus and his good news of the kingdom, we are doing what Jesus told us to do when he said, "All authority in heaven and earth has been given to me. Go therefore and make disciples of all nations, baptizing them in the name of the Father and of the Son and of the Holy Spirit, teaching them to observe all that I have commanded you. And behold, I am with you always, to the end of the age" (Matt. 28:18–20).

The good news of the kingdom is yours, and it is available for sharing with everyone everywhere.

CAN THE KINGDOM BE EXPLAINED BY QUANTUM THEORY?

Can the kingdom be explained by quantum theory? If I could clearly explain quantum theory, the answer would still probably remain a definite maybe. First, in quantum theory we deal with subatomic particles and energies. We cannot see these with the naked eye. I was first astonished by things that cannot be seen with the naked eye when I was quite a young child while using the family microscope and discovering wiggly things in water and red corpuscles in a drop of blood. This was a whole new world for me. This was a whole new world that until then was invisible to me. Quantum theory deals with things that cannot be seen with the naked eye but nevertheless can be shown mathematically and scientifically to exist. Some of these smaller-than-atom particles and energies you are already probably acquainted with: electrons, protons, neutrons, nuclei, quarks, photons, and others.

When speaking about what is invisible to the naked eye, such as particles and energies, I recall the words of the Nicene Creed, one of the three ecumenical creeds of the Christian Church, which says that we believe that God has made heaven and earth and all that is seen and unseen or visible and invisible. In quantum theory it is widely believed that we are speaking about what is invisible to the naked eye in the material world. Many scientists may not include in their inquiries such entities as the invisible spirit beings such as angels, demons, and the like familiar to theologians and laypersons in religious circles. Scientists would prefer to inquire into what is in some way materially observable. Unfortunately, what is studied in quantum theory has the unfortunate possibility of changing even by being observed. Tricky, isn't it?

In addition, quantum theory, in its study of subatomic particles, also suggests that such particles and energies could exist not only in one static place but also simultaneously in more than one locality. Although this may be true, it seems as strange and controversial as the legendary stories of bilocation or the doppelgänger phenomenon. Some religious and paranormal sources, such as Brian Haughton in his *Handbook of Paranormal Powers*, report such incidents. He relates that bilocation occurred in the lives of a number of "Christian saints, mystics, and monks, including St. Ambrose of Milan (338–397), St. Severus of Ravenna (born c. 348), St. Anthony of Padua (1195–1231), and St. Pio of Pietrelcina (also known as Padre Pio (1887–1968)." Such legends may be very difficult to verify with the familiar scientific method. If, however, subatomic particles and energies can actually exist bilocationally, in more than one place at the same time, in the microcosmic world of the lesser subatomic particles and energies, might this property also have an expression with things that exist in the greater-than-subatomic realm of the macrocosmic world? Such thoughts and questions can be applicable not only to the physical world but also to some questions in the spiritual realm. To me this may be not only simply an unusual inquiry but also one that is exciting and mind expanding.

The more quantum theory is studied, the more awesome discoveries about our world seem to be exposed.[2] The understanding of the realm of time and space is expanded. With respect to the subject of time, Einstein's theories have enabled us to understand time as being relative. His theories of time regarding space and matter together with his view of gravity have greatly expanded our understanding of the universe. When Einstein was confronted in the early days of quantum studies with the ideas of Heisenberg, Niels Bohr, and others, he wasn't all that impressed. Someone has said that, speaking about how fluid quantum theory affords a randomness and uncertainty in a probabilistic universe, Einstein once remarked, "Der Herrgott wurfelt nicht"—that is, "God does not throw dice."[3] Possibly, if he could be involved in what is being done today in the realm of quantum theory, he may alter some of his previous evaluations.

Quantum theory also opens up the real possibility of parallel universes or multiple dimensions. Think, *Thy kingdom come on earth as it is in heaven.* When Jesus taught in numerous parables that the kingdom of heaven was like something earthly, he was ruling out neither the earthly realm nor the heavenly realm. Rather, he said that the reality of the qualities of the kingdom could and even should simultaneously exist in both the earthly and heavenly dimensions.

There may, in fact, be many more than these two dimensions. In which kingdom dimension should we live? Should we be concerned only about our lives in the three-dimensional world with which we are familiar? With respect to the heavenly realm, we may have to wait until we pass from this earthly realm into the fullness of the heavenly realm when we die. The apostle speaks of an experience he had with these words.

> I will go on to visions and revelations of the Lord. I know a man in Christ who fourteen years ago was caught up to the third heaven—whether in the body or out of the body I do not know. God knows. And I know that this man was caught up into paradise—whether in the body or out of the body or out of the body I do not know, God knows—and he heard things that cannot be told, which man may not utter. On behalf of this man I will boast, but on my own behalf I will not boast, except of my weakness. (2 Cor. 12:1–5).

What is meant by these three heavens? The first heaven may refer to what we understand as everything in our earthly atmosphere: the air we breathe and where the birds of the air fly and where clouds float above us. The second heaven may be a reference to the starry heavens: the sun, the moon, the stars, and the various planets. The third heaven may be the dimension often referred to as the heaven of the blessed. Do the apostle's words indicate that there may indeed be other dimensions or that it may be possible for a person to have an extra-dimensional experience?

Quantum thinking can possibly also be extended into the realm of prayer. Prayer can be directed not only to what concerns us locally but also to circumstances and people who may be far away. I am reminded of how a person requested Jesus to heal his servant who was some distance away, and Jesus positively influenced the health of that person while being in a different place altogether than the object of healing (Matt. 8:5–13). It appears that Jesus could be active in what quantum theory would call "another dimension" or that he could operate transdimensionally—that is, across the dimensions. One person in a Bible class once remarked, "Oh, I get it. Jesus could heal by remote control, couldn't he?"

The internationally renowned Japanese scientist Masaru Emoto did some very intriguing experiments. His results were shared in his book *The Hidden Messages in Water*. He said, "The entire universe is in a state of vibration, and each thing generates its own frequency." He explained, "But now the science of quantum mechanics generally acknowledges that substance is nothing more than vibration. When we separate something into its smallest parts, we always enter a strange world where all that exists is particles and waves."[4] We know then that because everything vibrates, everything creates sound. We also know that sound such as music and words must be received into our ears for it to be heard. We have all heard the question "If a tree falls in a forest and there is no one around, does it make a sound?" Dr. Emoto says that with respect to all vibrations, "There is a *master listener* to receive the sound: water."[5]

Masaru Emoto's experiments with water showed that music, spoken words, and even written words on paper placed on the container of water were actually "received" by the water. He froze the water exposed to classical music and positive words such as *love* and *gratitude*. The frozen water formed beautiful, well-formed crystals. Water exposed to violent heavy metal music or negative words formed malformed frozen crystals. He shared photographs of each kind of crystal formations. His experiments certainly have shown that negative sounds and words have negative results and that positive words have positive results.

In addition, many miracles of Jesus, such as changing water into wine (John 2:11) and stilling the storm (Luke 8:22-25), and many other healings and miracles involve not only subatomic properties but also visible entities and physical forces. Can it be said that quantum theory also has a place in prayer and miracles? Am I saying that prayer and miracles can or should be explained using quantum theory? I don't think prayer, miracles, or any other religious teachings need to be, or even can be, adequately explained by reason or any scientific method. I do think quantum theory and other theories, such as the use of reason and scientific methods, can help us to be more able to appreciate the things of faith and of the whole creation. There is the realm of faith or trust, and there is the realm of the material. Shall we think these realms we are familiar with and those we aren't familiar will never interface with each other? I believe that God's creation is more complex than we now are aware. I believe in the value of science. I believe in miracles. Can you see the bird's nest in my mustard tree?

The Good News of the Kingdom

How does quantum theory help us to understand the good news of the kingdom Jesus proclaimed? It is somewhat like saying, "Can you see the bird's nest in my mustard tree?" There are many earthly things in our natural world that aren't always easily seen, but they nevertheless actually exist. When Jesus spoke of the kingdom in many of his parables, he used earthly things and circumstances to express certain spiritual truths that exist in the kingdom that cannot always be easily seen.

We sometimes need to be reminded that, even though we cannot always easily see or understand spiritual truths pertaining to God and our lives, we can trust that God who created us and all things wants what is best for us. The Bible reminds us, "Now faith is the assurance of things hoped for, the conviction of things not seen" (Heb. 11:1). This is true, even when we cannot always easily see the reality in our physical lives now or how God is involved in our lives for our eternal welfare. The good news is that God knows not only all about quantum reality; he also knows each of us better than we know ourselves. He sees the bird's nest in our mustard tree. That's the good news about the kingdom.

THE KINGDOM WITHIN

When we speak of the kingdom Jesus proclaimed, we do well to remember that the kingdom and the person of Jesus can be separated only with great difficulty. Where Jesus is, there is the kingdom. Wherever the kingdom is, there is Jesus. At one point Jesus cast a demon out of a man. Some of the Pharisees accused him of using demonic power to accomplish this feat. Jesus asked, "And if Satan casts out Satan, he is divided against himself. How then will his kingdom stand? ... But if it is by the Spirit of God that I cast out demons, then the kingdom of God has come upon you" (Matt. 12:26–28). On another occasion the Bible tells us, "Jesus came into Galilee, proclaiming the gospel of God, and saying, 'The time is fulfilled, and the kingdom of God is at hand; repent and believe the gospel'" (Mark 1:14–15). A number of times Jesus said, "Repent, the kingdom of heaven is at hand" (Matt. 3:2; 4:17). I believe that when

Jesus used the expression "at hand" when speaking of the kingdom, he said that the kingdom is as present or as close as he is present.

The kingdom is also associated with the condition of one's heart. Repentance includes one's sorrow or contrition of one's sinful condition, and it trusts God for the forgiveness of sin. Jesus forgives sin. Jesus is the King of the kingdom wherein there is forgiveness (Luke 5:17–26; 23:34). Wherever Jesus is, there is the kingdom. Wherever the kingdom is, there is forgiveness. The good news of the kingdom is that wherever Jesus is, the kingdom with all its blessings is present, at hand, as near as one's very fingertips.

Jesus also spoke of the kingdom as being present with these words. "Being asked by the Pharisees when the kingdom of God would come, he answered them, 'The kingdom of God is not coming with signs to be observed, nor will they say, "Look, here it is!" or "There!" for behold, the kingdom of God is in the midst of you'" (Luke 17:20–21). Jesus here told us that the kingdom of God is within or inside us. People who have Jesus in their hearts have the kingdom in the midst of them. The kingdom is in us, and we are in the kingdom. Where Jesus is, there is the kingdom.

In the noncanonical gnostic Gospel of Thomas, which purports to record some of the sayings of Jesus, we read that Jesus said, "If your leaders say to you, 'Look, the kingdom is in heaven,' then the birds of heaven will precede you. If they say to you, 'It is in the sea,' then the fish will precede you. Rather, the kingdom is inside you, and it is outside you"[6] (Gos. Thom., Saying 3). The Gnostics were members of a religious-philosophical sect that existed in several forms, even before Christ and during the early centuries after Christ. Most Gnostics claimed that the material-physical world is evil and that spirit alone is good, but people could be saved with their secret knowledge.

The very first saying in the Gospel of Thomas attributed to Jesus states, "Whoever discovers the interpretation of these sayings will not taste death." The word *gnostic* is derived from the Greek word *gnosis*, which is translated as "knowledge." Their secret knowledge wasn't what Christians teach as faith in Jesus the Messiah; instead it consisted of a mental or intellectual understanding of various teachings. Another saying from the Gospel of Thomas about the kingdom reports, "His followers said to him, 'When will the kingdom come?' It will not come by watching for it. It will not be said, 'Look, here it is,' or 'Look, there it is.' Rather, the father's kingdom is spread out upon the earth, and people do not see it"[7] (Gos. Thom., Saying 113).

The above-mentioned sayings 3 and 113 from the Gospel of Thomas sound on the surface to be quite similar to the quotes of Jesus as reported in the Bible. The difference lies in the underlying context of the gnostic teaching. These gnostic sayings are understood best within the context of their intellectual or mental secret knowledge. The gnostic concept of the kingdom also rests on an intellectual knowledge and understanding of the kingdom. When a person reaches what might be called a kind of intellectual enlightenment, he or she can be said to have attained *gnosis*, and it is then that one experiences the kingdom.

In the Bible these gnostic sayings of Jesus rest on the context of one's connection with Jesus through faith and trust in him as their Savior and King. People who by faith have Jesus within their hearts participate wholly in the kingdom and its blessings, which Jesus proclaimed. Unlike the gnostic concept of secret mental knowledge, the Christian's faith isn't dependent on one's knowledge, intellectual enlightenment, or understanding. Knowledge is of the head, whereas faith and trust are of the heart.

In the New Testament letter to Timothy, the apostle warned Timothy, saying, "O Timothy, guard the deposit entrusted to you. Avoid the irreverent babble and contradictions of what is falsely called 'knowledge [gnosis],' for by professing it some have swerved from the faith" (1 Tim. 6:20). When the Bible says the kingdom is in the midst of you, it refers to the kingdom that rests on one's simple inner faith of the heart.

THE GOOD NEWS OF THE KINGDOM

The Christian faith applauds God's gift of human intellectual powers and activity. Neither the teachings of Jesus nor the formal teachings of the Christian church equate intellectual powers and activity with faith. Neither one's intellectual understanding nor the extent of one's knowledge of the Bible is what qualifies a person's entrance into the kingdom Jesus proclaimed. It is one's faith that is the criteria for entrance into the kingdom. This is why Jesus referenced one's faith when he said, "The time is fulfilled, and the kingdom of God is at hand; repent and believe in the gospel" (Mark 1:15).

I am personally happy that one's intellectual status or powers aren't the measure God uses for determining one's suitability for entrance into the kingdom. If one's intellectual powers were the criteria for entrance into the kingdom, I may not be smart enough for entering and participating in the kingdom Jesus proclaimed. Instead, I'm simply placing my faith and trust in Jesus. I want to be with Jesus, who is the King of his kingdom. When Jesus is by faith residing within, or in the midst of, my innermost being of heart, there also I am with him in his kingdom. His kingdom is within me, and I am within his kingdom. When I die, I want to hear what King Jesus said to the criminal of the cross. "Truly, I say to you, today you will be with me in Paradise [the king's garden]" (Luke 23:43). That's good news. That's the good news of his kingdom. Can you see the bird's nest in my mustard tree?

Chapter 6

THE KINGDOM
HIGHLIGHTS LOVE

AT THIS POINT I am first returning to the area of the Sea of Galilee at the town of Capernaum. It is in this vicinity that Jesus called his first disciples and began his public ministry. It is here that he said, "I must preach the good news of the kingdom of God to the other towns as well; for I was sent for this purpose" (Luke 4:43).

We have seen some of the aspects of what this "good news of the kingdom of God" includes. We have indicated a number of these aspects because it was difficult for some at that time and even now to grasp what Jesus meant by the gospel or good news of the kingdom. He didn't proclaim his death on the cross and resurrection from the dead, since this didn't happen until the last part of his earthly ministry. He did, however, predict that it would be necessary for him to suffer and die; this is mentioned three times in all the synoptic gospels. Throughout his ministry, Jesus expressed what he meant by the "good news of the kingdom" not only through his verbal proclamations but also through his actions.

The good news of the kingdom includes the concept of presence. The presence of Jesus himself is central to understanding the good news of the kingdom. Jesus himself put it this way: "The kingdom of God is at hand" (Matt. 4:17). When and where Jesus is at hand, the kingdom of God is "at hand," as near as one's fingertips. Where Jesus is, there is the kingdom. The concept of presence is well within the scriptural context of God's presence, as indicated in the life of Joseph and his brothers as well as throughout the lives of the patriarchs, judges, kings, and prophets. The presence of God is shown to be lovingly providential and supportive within the understanding of the gospel or good news of the kingdom.

The good news of the kingdom is also evident in the love demonstrated through the many healings, exorcisms, and miracles of Jesus. God's goodness, open acceptance, patience, loving grace, and justice are seen in the kingdom parables of Jesus. The good news of the kingdom is a message that assures us that God is in control, even, and perhaps especially, when the circumstances of life seem so out of control. The kingdom of God Jesus proclaimed is a kingdom where one's faith and trust in King Jesus brings hope into one's life and the assurance of God's love.

At this point I want to mention a significant word in the proclamation of Jesus when he said, "Repent, for the kingdom of heaven is at hand" (Matt. 4:17). Notice the first word, *repent*. This concept of repentance is intimately connected with the rest of the statement, which speaks about his presence being "at hand" with respect to the kingdom. Unfortunately, there is an incomplete understanding among many concerning what repentance includes. Many associate the idea of being sorry for one's sins as being nearly equivalent to what it means to repent. Yes, being sorry or having remorse over one's sins, or having contrition, is certainly included in what it means to repent. Others will include making restitution for your sins as much as that is humanly possible. So far all this sounds good.

Repentance certainly includes making a change of direction, or a turnaround, in one's thinking and acting. It is receiving the power from God to believe—that is, to trust that you are forgiven of your former sinful way of life and that you can now, with God's power in your life, change your way of thinking and behaving. Repentance includes the law of God, which shows us the sin for which we need to have contrition, but it also includes the gospel, which shows us the love and forgiveness God extends.[1] With this belief and faith, you can now go forward toward a new way of life, trusting that God has forgiven you and continually strengthens you to fulfill your life's purpose. We are seeing in the expression "repent" the process of change that includes thinking, belief, or trust, and what is often referred to as "conversion."

When Jesus calls people to repentance, he calls them to change the direction of their lives by leaving their old way of life and entering a new way of life as they come into his loving and forgiving presence in his kingdom. Repentance is the process of sorrow or contrition that moves toward changing from living apart from Jesus to living with him. As you live with him in faith and trust, you will receive his blessings of the forgiveness of sins and a life that enjoys his loving presence as the king or ruler of your life in his kingdom. Jesus wants this for all people, and that is why he calls people to "repent, for the kingdom of heaven is at hand." Jesus loves everyone so much that he calls all to repentance so they might enjoy being in his presence in his kingdom.

Jesus said, "A new commandment I give to you, that you love one another; just as I have loved you, you also are to love one another. By this all people will know that you are my disciples, if you have love for one another" (John 13:34–35). It may seem strange that Jesus commands people to love. How can love be commanded?

When most of us think of love, we think of feelings. Most people understand that feelings cannot be commanded to exist. The kind of love Jesus commanded isn't simply the feelings we so often associate with love. This isn't to say that the love Jesus commanded might also include certain feelings. Feelings aren't necessarily bad. The love Jesus commanded isn't bad, nor is it the popular romantic kind of feeling. It may be good at this point to review the various ways the word *love* is used.

Truly the understanding of love in the English language is quite broad. The one word *love* can mean anything from having romantic love to describing how much a person has a passion for chocolate. In the language of the New Testament, various words are used to more accurately describe the various kinds of love.[2] The Greek word *philia* refers to brotherly love. It is also part of the word *Philadelphia*, which is often referred to as the city of brotherly love. Another Greek word is *storge*, which is used when speaking of familial love. This is the love parents have for their children and which children have for their parents and brothers and sisters.

Another word used for love in the New Testament is *agape*. This is a more perfect kind of love, which describes the disposition a person has when he or she serves others. This is a love that is willing to sacrifice oneself for the benefit of another. Agape is the kind of love that describes how Jesus loved and served others. We see it in its ultimate sense of sacrificial service when we see Jesus offering himself on the cross to save all humanity. It is a love that prompts a person to help and serve others, and expects nothing in return. It is a love that desires not to receive from others but to give to others.

In a conversation Jesus had with Simon Peter, he used both forms of agape and *philia*. Twice Jesus asked Peter whether he loved him with an agape love. Twice Peter responded that he loved him with a *philia* kind of love. Finally, Jesus asked Peter whether he loved him with a *philia* kind of love. Peter was grieved that Jesus used the *philia* kind of love in his third questioning, for then he realized that, although his love was a noble brotherly love, it wasn't as intense or pure as is incorporated in the word *agape* (John 21:15–17). I believe Jesus used this event to encourage all of us to have the disposition or inclination to live in love toward him and one another with the kind of agape love he also has shown to us.

Another Greek word *eros* isn't used in the New Testament but describes a more sensual or passionate kind of love. The Septuagint, often abbreviated as LXX, is a Greek translation of the Hebrew Bible dating back to 285–247 BC by seventy or seventy-two Jewish scholars at Alexandria. This translation came into use especially because Greek had become the *linguae francae* or widely understood language of the Mediterranean world and was popular among Jews during the Dispersion and also by the early Christian missionaries. The LXX uses the word *eros* in its translation of Proverbs 7:18.[3] An English derivative of *eros* is the word *erotic*. This is the love that includes our physical and sexual attraction to others. This isn't in itself necessarily a sinful attraction, but it is part of the natural human condition with which we have all been created. The Song of Solomon makes reference to such a love between a husband and wife, which could also be compared to the love God has for his people without using the word *eros*. Although this may be true, eros is a powerful physical, human condition that frequently can be used sinfully only to selfishly please oneself.

When Jesus said, "Love one another just as I have loved you," he was calling us to love one another with the highest form of love. In Matthew 19:19, he quoted the Old Testament, saying, "You shall love your neighbor as yourself" (Lev. 19:18). Have you noticed the difference? In the Old Testament quotation, a person should love another as the person loves himself or herself, but now Jesus said that we should love one another "*just as I have loved you*" (my own italics). Our love should be compared to the love Jesus has shown to us. There is no contradiction here of the love Jesus advocated and what is stated in the Old Testament. It is a matter of emphasis.

When Jesus met with his disciples for the last Passover supper they would have together, he stooped down to wash the disciples' feet. The washing of the feet in those days wasn't just a symbolic action. It was a necessity because people walked almost everywhere they went. With the kind of shoes or sandals they wore, their feet would have become quite dusty rather quickly. Now Jesus stooped to wash the disciples' feet.

Peter objected because he thought it was improper for a master to condescend to wash a lowly disciple's feet, but Jesus insisted. He said, "Do you understand what I have done to you? You call me Teacher and Lord, and you are right, for so I am. If I then, your Lord and Teacher, have washed your feet, you also ought to wash one another's feet. For I have given you an example, that you also should do just as I have done to you" (John 13:12–15). Jesus loved his disciples so much that he served them in this way, even if it meant humbling himself. The lesson of love Jesus exemplified in this activity was simply that love serves. "A new commandment I give to you, that you love one another; just as I have loved you, you also are to love one another. By this all people will know that you are my disciples, if you have love for one another" (John 13:34–35).

Jesus also demonstrated his love when he served the people of the world by sacrificially dying for everyone on the cross. When Jesus made this comparison, he went on to explain this kind of love by saying, "Greater love has no one than this, that someone lays down his life for his friends. You are my friends if you do what I command you" (John 15:13–14). Now the comparison isn't just with how much we love ourselves, which may not always be perfect, but our love is now to be compared to the love of the sinless Son of God, who loved everyone perfectly, even unto death.

The intensity of the suffering and death of Jesus demonstrates to us the depths of his love. His suffering was more than physical. His suffering also included mental, emotional, and spiritual suffering. When Jesus was betrayed, this came by one of his own disciples. When Jesus was captured, his disciples forsook him and fled. The Bible tells us, "So the band of soldiers and their captain and the officers of the Jews arrested Jesus and bound him" (John 18:12). Just think; here is the Son of God himself who could have easily destroyed them all with a word and now permitted himself to be bound. He went with them willingly. As Isaiah wrote, "He was oppressed, and he was afflicted, yet he opened not his mouth; like a lamb that is led to the slaughter, and like a sheep that before its shearers is silent, so he opened not his mouth" (Isa. 53:7).

One of his disciples Peter denied that he had ever known Jesus. Jesus was humiliated, both at a religious trial before the high priest and before the civil authority Pontius Pilate. They took away his clothes and dressed him in a kingly garment. They made a crown out of thorns, which was put on his head. They placed a stick for a scepter in his hand and mocked him as a king. It is said that this was done as the Roman soldiers played the game of the king. There are places in Jerusalem where marks still exist in the stone floors, such as is found at the Ecce Homo Convent, where the soldiers played such a game.

Jesus was flogged. This was a punishment so severe that his body was striped with the bloody marks of the whip. The end of each cord or leather lash of the whip often contained leaded balls, bone, or other weights, which, when striking the skin, would inflict deep wounds. Some victims of flogging came close to death or even died. Such treatment not only physically brutalized Jesus's body but certainly also caused him much mental and emotional pain. In such a physically tortured condition, Jesus was then compelled to carry his own cross to a hill called Golgotha or Calvary outside the city walls to be crucified. He was placed on the cross, and nails were pounded through his hands and feet to fasten him to the cross.

While Jesus hung on the cross, he cried out, "'Eli, Eli, lema sabachthani?"—that is, 'My God, my God, why have you forsaken me?" (Matt. 27:46). This saying of Jesus, which he quoted from Psalm 22:1, has much meaning for me. One of the greatest torments a person experiences in hell is being completely forsaken and separated from God. Here on earth we can all take comfort in the fact that God is always with us and loves and cares for us. In hell there is no such comfort; a person is completely separated and forsaken of God's loving presence. When Jesus spoke those words—"My God, my God, why have you forsaken me?"—he not only experienced the physical torments of an earthly crucifixion; he also experienced the torments of hell itself. He endured all this willingly, suffering the punishment of hell itself for us. He suffered not because he himself had any sin for which to suffer, but he suffered the torments of hell for us on the cross so we wouldn't have to ever suffer the forsakenness of hell because of our sinfulness.

The intensity of suffering Jesus endured through his life, his suffering and death, shows us clearly the great depth of love he has for each one of us. We deserve hell because of our sins, but his love for us frees us from the punishment of being forsaken by God in hell and enables us to live in his loving presence forever. "For the wages of sin is death, but the free gift of God is eternal life in Christ Jesus our Lord" (Rom. 6:23). What a great love Jesus has for us! "For God so loved the world, that he gave his only Son, that whoever believes in him should not perish but have eternal life. For God did not send his Son into the world to condemn the world, but in order that the world might be saved through him" (John 3:16–17).

We should now love God and one another just as God loves us. Jesus said, "A new commandment I give to you, that you love one another; just as I have loved you, you also are to love one another" (John 13:34). The Bible also says, "Beloved, let us love one another, for love is from God, and whoever loves has been born of God and knows God. Anyone who does not love does not know God, because God is love" (1 John 4:7–8). God is described as love itself. Can any of us describe ourselves as love itself? Hardly! Love isn't often understood as a being. If God is understood as a being, he can here be understood as the being of love.

This portion of scripture reveals how God made his love shown. "In this the love of God was made manifest among us, that God sent his only Son into the world, so that we might live though him. In this is love, not that we have loved God but that he loved us and sent his Son to be the propitiation for our sins. Beloved, if God so loved us, we also ought to love one another" (1 John 4:9–12).

In one of the Bible classes I was leading, the subject of how we should show love to one another was being discussed. One of the participants said we show love to one another by being kind to others. I suppose I was expecting what might be described as a more theological comment and was rather surprised by the simplicity of the answer. The more I thought about that answer, the more profound it has become to me. I suppose I was experiencing the question "Can you see the bird's nest in my mustard tree?" What a wonderful world it would be if everyone could only be kind to one another. Couldn't that be described as a more loving world?

The prophet Micah once made a statement that has become one of my favorite passages in his book. "What does the Lord require of you but to do justice, and to love kindness, and to walk humbly with your God?" (Mic. 6:8). What a beautiful disposition of love to possess and what a delightful way to express love to others. I suppose we could all ask ourselves how kind and loving we are to others.

The gospel of the kingdom Jesus proclaimed truly shows that the kingdom highlights a new commandment, as he said, "Love one another just as I have loved you."

> Love is a disposition,
>
> Always to be
>
> Unconditionally
>
> For others,
>
> Never against them,
>
> Genuinely
>
> Accepting one another
>
> in joy,
>
> Overflowing
>
> with kindness and gentleness.

Chapter 7

A KINGDOM FOR THE ORDINARY

I ONCE HEARD criticism about a person who was involved in so many Bible study programs and pursued such an intense personal prayer regimen that it was said of him that he was so heavenly minded that he was no earthly good. At times I wonder if some people don't feel that way about God. Is God so busy with the really big problems of other people and of the great nations of the world that we shouldn't bother him with our everyday, ordinary problems, which in comparison may seem so much smaller and of lesser importance? Is the kingdom Jesus proclaimed really for ordinary people with ordinary problems? One of the best ways to answer that question is to observe the King of the kingdom, Jesus himself.

Jesus was walking by the Sea of Galilee and called Peter and Andrew, and also James and John, to be his disciples. They were fishermen. These men weren't the elite of society. They caught fish for a living (Matt. 4:18–22). They were ordinary men involved in an ordinary, albeit a rather rough and tumble, occupation. Most of the disciples of Jesus were ordinary people. Matthew was also called to be a disciple. He was a Jewish tax collector for the despised Roman government, and because of this, he was thought of as a sinner and traitor to his people, yet Jesus called him to be counted among the twelve disciples

(Matt. 10:2–4). Jesus didn't think of himself as being too important or too special to associate with ordinary people, even if that person might be considered an outcast or a notorious sinner. Jesus also called Judas to be a disciple, even though he later betrayed him. Jesus surrounded himself with people of all kinds and descriptions. His is the kingdom for the ordinary. The King of the kingdom is for all people.

Jesus not only identified with the common people but also showed his concern for their ordinary needs. The evangelist John told us about a time when Jesus went up on the mountain with his disciples. A large crowd gathered around him. "Jesus said to Philip, 'Where are we to buy bread, so that these people may eat?'" (John 6:5). Although Jesus may have known what to do, the question itself indicates that Jesus recognized a very ordinary need the people had. They were hungry. They needed food. As we read what transpired, we see that Jesus, the King of the kingdom, used five loaves of bread and two fish to miraculously feed five thousand people. Jesus was not only concerned about the ordinary needs of people; he was also the provider of those needs.

We can trust Jesus to provide for our ordinary needs. Does this mean we don't need to do anything to obtain our food? The New Testament says, "If anyone is not willing to work, let him not eat. For we hear that some among you walk in idleness, not busy at work, but busybodies. Now such persons we command and encourage in the Lord Jesus Christ to do their work quietly and to earn their own living" (2 Thess. 3:10–12). Jesus does provide for our ordinary needs, but as we trust him, we are expected to do what we can to earn our own living. Will Jesus provide for our ordinary needs by doing a miracle like he did for the five thousand on the mountain? Perhaps. That method of meeting needs is always a possibility, but in the meantime, we are encouraged to recognize our own responsibility to provide for our ordinary needs, which is to work to earn our own living.

There is another ordinary responsibility people are required to fulfill. Sometimes this responsibility is frequently expressed by saying that there are only two certainties we can always count on, and these are death and taxes. It's best to let God be the One in charge of the inevitability of our deaths, but while we are alive, it is necessary for us to deal with the obligation of paying our taxes. There was a time when some people came to Jesus, asking, "'Is it lawful to pay taxes to Caesar, or not?' But, knowing their hypocrisy, he said to them, 'Why put me to the test? Bring me a denarius and let me look at it.' And they brought one. And he said to them, 'Whose likeness and inscription is this?' They said to him, 'Caesar's.' Jesus said to them, 'Render to Caesar the things that are Caesar's, and to God the things that are God's.' And they marveled at him" (Mark 12:14–17).

It is apparent that these questioners had hoped to catch Jesus either denouncing Caesar or demeaning God. Instead he gave an answer that could be understood as supporting both Caesar and God. They were amazed. Certainly among the things that were Caesar's was the authority to impose taxes. The question now remained as to what constituted the things that were God's. I immediately thought of the first words in the Gospel of John: "In the beginning was the Word, and the Word was with God, and the Word was God. He was in the beginning with God. All things were made through him, and without him was not any thing made that was made" (John 1:1–3). God made all things. Everything made belongs to God. When Jesus said, "Render … to God the things that are God's," was he not also saying that everything should be rendered to God? If the questioners understood that basic fact, it is no wonder that they marveled. Even ordinary things, such as paying taxes and acknowledging that all things belong to God, are included in the good news of the kingdom Jesus proclaimed.

One thing common to all people is that they have all had a mother enabling them to come into the world. Jesus was a true man. He was also true God. He came into the world as an ordinary human baby born in the town of Bethlehem of his mother, Mary. This process of God becoming a human being theologians call "the incarnation." Christians celebrate this wondrous incarnational event every year at Christmas. We don't really know whether Jesus was born on December 25. His birth could have taken place just as well sometime in the spring, summer, or autumn. The importance of the event isn't when it happened; it's that God became a human being in the person of Jesus. Merry Christmas!

Why would God want to clothe himself in an ordinary human body and come to live on earth? Some people even think human bodies are bad. One person said, "If I just didn't have my body to contend with, I could almost live a perfect life." But now the holy God himself took upon himself an ordinary human body to accomplish something very important.

God certainly doesn't think of the ordinary human body as bad. He is the One who originally created human bodies when he created Adam and Eve in the Garden of Eden. God likes human bodies. When the human race became exceptionally wicked, he saved eight humans in Noah's ark when the great deluge occurred. All eight had human bodies. God likes human bodies. At his birth, he took upon himself an ordinary human body. He likes ordinary human bodies.

God has given all of us a body. We should not despise it. We should care for it, not abuse it, and use it to carry out what God has intended for us to do. We need to care for one another's common bodily welfare. When Jesus was dying on the cross, he looked down and saw his mother at the foot of the cross together with the disciple whom he loved. He wanted her to be cared for bodily. He said, "'Woman, behold your son!' Then he said to the disciple, 'Behold, your mother!' And from that hour the disciple took her to his own home" (John 19:26–27).

God's purpose for becoming a human was because he loves everyone no matter what our bodies look like. He loves all people no matter what one's status is. God loves everyone, whether one is among those who are thought of as ordinary or among those thought of as the elite. God considers everyone as equals. The apostle Peter said, "Truly I understand that God shows no partiality, but in every nation anyone who fears him and does what is right is acceptable to him" (Acts 10:34–35).

Put yourself in God's place. When you love someone, you want the best for him or her. He saw that all people had really become wicked. He loved all with a perfect love. He didn't want to wipe them off the face of the earth, so he came down to earth as an ordinary human, yet without sin, so that he might save them from the eternal consequences of their wickedness. He came to live a perfect life of love for all humanity so that people might know that God truly loves and cares for them. People could best see this love of God as God bodily lived that perfect life of love among them.

Jesus lived that perfect life of love among ordinary people as he taught, served, and saved us through his life, death, and resurrection. Now he wants us to follow him by loving, serving, teaching, and giving of ourselves in every way so that other ordinary people might come to trust in him as their Lord as they become his saved people. Can you see the bird's nest in my mustard tree? God's kingdom is for ordinary people so that all might live with an extraordinary King who came to earth to love every one of us with a perfect love.

Chapter 8

THE KINGDOM OF HEALING

As a pastor, I have visited many individuals who were sick. So often I have heard the question, "What have I done to deserve this?" The belief that sickness and injury are a way God punishes people for their sins is alive and well, even among some faithful Christians. It is true, on the other hand, that many illnesses *are* the result of years of bad health habits, substance abuse, or injury from others. Rather than blaming our illnesses and misfortunes on God, it may be that at times we are the ones more responsible for how we have mistreated our bodies.

At the time of Jesus, it was common to believe God's punishment for the commission of specific sins was suffering illness or enduring physical deformities and debilitating conditions. Jesus rejected such a belief. His disciples once asked him whether a certain man who was born blind suffered this condition because he or his parents had sinned. Jesus answered, "It was not that this man sinned, or his parents, but that the works of God might be displayed in him" (John 9:1–3). Jesus then healed the man of his blindness.

When Jesus proclaimed the gospel of the kingdom, his proclamation was not only with words but also through the healing of those suffering from various diseases and infirmities. The Bible tells us, "And he went throughout all Galilee, teaching in their synagogues and proclaiming the gospel of the kingdom and healing every disease and every affliction among the people" (Matt. 4:23). Why did Jesus choose healing as a means to proclaim what the gospel of the kingdom was all about? Jesus met the people where they were. He wanted to meet the needs of the people. The people themselves and their families mostly took care of the heath care of the people. There were people in the communities who became known as those who were more skilled in providing help to the sick. The priests were considered the final arbitrators about what constituted a healing, especially regarding skin diseases such as leprosy.

A physician class could hardly be said to exist among the Israelites. The evangelist Luke was considered a physician, perhaps indicating a Greek influence. Even the best of care was meager among the Hebrews compared to what we have available today. They couldn't simply go down to the corner pharmacy and buy a bottle of aspirin. For people with simple infections incurred because of a lack of basic hygiene, a minor cut could become deadly. The overall need for medical care was great. In addition to the extensive need for medical care, Jesus saw not only the disease or condition but also the individual. Jesus was concerned with the whole person. It is interesting that in the Greek language of the New Testament the word for both *healer* and *savior* is the same. As a healer Jesus was concerned about the total care of an individual, the body *and* soul.

We see God's healing love throughout the time the children of Israel spent after the exodus from Egypt as they went through the wilderness. Recall the incident in Numbers 21:4–9 when the people spoke against God and Moses, and then encountered an attack of poisonous serpents. The serpents helped to prompt the people to

once again return to God and accept the leadership of Moses. God
told Moses, "'Make a fiery serpent and set it on a pole, and everyone
who is bitten, when he sees it, shall live.' So Moses made a bronze
serpent and set it on a pole. And if a serpent bit anyone, they would
look at the bronze serpent and live" (Num. 21:4-9). This was actually
a healing and saving event a loving God provided to a rebellious
people. Jesus referenced this healing event, which saved those whom
serpents bit, when he said, "And as Moses lifted up the serpent in
the wilderness, so must the Son of Man be lifted up, that whoever
believes in him may have eternal life" (John 3:14).

That a serpent would be associated with the healing in the wilderness
and with the healing and saving ministry of Jesus may seem strange
to us. Many people now think of the snake in a more negative light.
The serpent in the creation narrative is thought of more as a satanic
and destructive entity rather than a helpful one. Some snakes are
venomous, and their bites are dangerous.

Serpents were often associated with ideas and beliefs in ancient times
regarding immortality, regeneration, and healing for many of the
ancient people. For example, the symbol of a serpent and staff related
to the Greek god Asclepius, who was known as a god of healing and
medicine. A shrine for Asclepius was excavated as part of the Pool
of Bethesda site in Jerusalem.[1] Jesus healed a paralytic at this shrine
(John 5:2–14). To attend this shrine for healing would have been
thought of as idolatrous. This may explain the words of Jesus to the
healed paralytic: "See, you are well! Sin no more, that nothing worse
may happen to you" (John 5:14).

The symbol for the medical and healing profession today is the
caduceus, which represents two serpents twined around the winged
staff of the Greek god Hermes. When Jesus likened himself to the

serpent Moses lifted up in the wilderness, he portrayed himself as a healing and saving person. When Jesus incorporated healing in his ministry, he proclaimed the caring love of God through these healing and regenerative saving actions. As we know, Jesus was finally lifted up on a cross to accomplish the healing and saving of all people (Isa. 53:4-5; John 15:13; John 19:16–30; Cor. 5:14–15; 1 Peter 2:24). The gospel of the kingdom Jesus proclaimed was nothing less than proclaiming the love of God to all the people of the world. God doesn't hate his own human creation. He isn't against them. God loves them with his perfect and unconditional love. As people receive God's loving and healing presence, they can be understood to be experiencing the very kingdom Jesus proclaimed to the people throughout his earthly ministry. Can you see the bird's nest in my mustard tree?

JESUS EXPRESSED AN IMPORTANT KEY TO THE KINGDOM

In his very person, Jesus expressed God's love not only in his words but especially also in action through his healing ministry. This is seen most clearly in his proclamation of forgiveness in connection with healing. An important aspect of healing is forgiveness. Forgiveness is one of the most loving and healing events a person can experience.

During one of the instances of his healing, he also proclaimed forgiveness to a paralyzed man. He said to the man, "My son, your sins are forgiven." Some scribes from the temple establishment thought this declaration of forgiveness was speaking blasphemy. In their minds, forgiveness could be obtained from God only through temple activities. Jesus said, "Why do you question these things in your hearts? Which is easier, to say to the paralytic, 'Your sins are forgiven,' or to say, 'Rise, take up your bed and walk'? But that you.

may know that the Son of Man has authority on earth to forgive sins'—he said to the paralytic—'I say to you, rise, pick up your bed and go home.' And he rose and immediately picked up his bed and went out before them all, so that they were all amazed and glorified God, saying, 'We never saw anything like this!'" (Mark 2:8–12).

Jesus proclaimed the gospel of the kingdom through his own person by granting the forgiveness of sins and healing. The kingdom of God is truly at hand in the person of Jesus. The kingdom is right here, as close as our fingertips, enabling us to live in a state of forgiveness as the presence of Jesus in this way is actively present with us. The great sixteenth-century reformer of the church Dr. Martin Luther once wrote in his small catechism, "Where there is forgiveness of sins there is also life and salvation."[2] During our lives with God now and in the life after death, forgiveness is the healing key that opens the door to actually be in and experience the gospel of the kingdom, which Jesus proclaimed. That's good news.

Crowds of people came to hear Jesus declare and exhibit in practical ways what the gospel of the kingdom was all about. The kingdom he spoke about and showed to them through his message of hope and his marvelous and healing deeds was better than the miserable existence they were experiencing. To me it is obvious that this is why so many followed him. He truly brought to them what he called the "gospel of the kingdom."

THE KINGDOM'S COMPASSIONATE KING

When Jesus healed, he indicated that he was truly concerned about the physical and spiritual welfare of the whole person. His healing proclaimed what the good news of the kingdom was all about.

The Gospel of Matthew tells us, "Jesus went on from there and walked beside the Sea of Galilee. And he went up on the mountain and sat down there. And great crowds came to him bringing with them the lame, the blind, the crippled, the mute and many others, and they put them at his feet, and he healed them, so that the crowd wondered, when they saw the mute speaking the crippled healthy, the lame walking and the blind seeing. And they glorified the God of Israel" (Matt. 15:29–31).

King Jesus was concerned about the physical and spiritual welfare of the whole person. We not only see a marvelous act; we also get a glimpse into the kind of heart Jesus had for people. The Bible tells us, "When he went ashore he saw a great crowd, and he had compassion on them and healed their sick" (Matt. 14:14). The good news of the kingdom is that Jesus, the King of the kingdom, has a heart for his people. He doesn't set himself aloof but permits the people to gather around him as he compassionately ministers to their needs.

Even today people seem able to sense whether their physician sees more than a disease and also truly cares about them as people. When a physician has only an unfeeling, clinical attitude, the patient senses this, even if the physician is otherwise very competent in his or her field of expertise. The physician's bedside manner actually has as much to do with conquering disease or disability as his or her ability to treat the person with medications and surgery. Jesus showed he was a compassionate healer. The good news of the kingdom is that in the kingdom there is compassion. This also means we who are in the kingdom also need to reflect the compassion of Jesus as we interact with others.

The healings Jesus accomplished seem to be of the more instantaneous healing than the healing that takes more time. As such, it may be difficult to classify the healing as a miracle rather than simply to identify it as a healing. It seems to me that most of the healings mentioned in the Bible could be classified as miraculous healings. Could Jesus still grant people miraculous healings? Of course! He could also grant people a healing that takes a longer period. Jesus also works through medicine, surgery, and other medical applications. He accomplishes the healing itself. The psalmist said, "Bless the Lord, O my soul, and forget not all his benefits, who forgives all your iniquity, who heals all your diseases" (Ps. 103:2–3). Jesus is still ministering to our bodies and souls. He still provides healing of our innermost souls by forgiving our sins and providing healing for our bodies. He is our great physician.

But wait; doesn't the psalm say, "Heals all your diseases?" Why, then, aren't all diseases healed? Think of it this way; all the diseases that are healed are healed by God. None are healed without God. True, we don't always experience the healing of all diseases. The apostle Paul, for example, had some physical malady about which he prayed to be healed. He put it this way: "Three times I pleaded with the Lord about this, that it should leave me. But he said to me, 'My grace is sufficient for you, for my power is made perfect in weakness'" (2 Cor. 12:8–9). God knows not only what we want but what in his wisdom is best for us, others, and his kingdom. In the meantime, be assured that in our weakness God's power will be able to work even better what is best for all.

The good news of the kingdom Jesus proclaimed through his healing ministry shows us a kingdom where mercy and compassion are openly available. In his kingdom, Jesus expressed his compassionate love through the healing of our whole being. Truly, the gospel of the kingdom is a kingdom of healing for both body and soul.

THE KINGDOM OF MIRACLES

OUR FAMILY WAS on a summer vacation in New Mexico. We were visiting many of the historic, picturesque churches and interesting art galleries in the Santa Fe and Taos areas. One evening we went to look at the famous St. Francis church at Ranchos de Taos, which artist Georgia O'Keeffe and other celebrated artists had painted because of its unusual architectural configuration. While we were there, we observed a painting; when it is seen in the darkness, a figure of Jesus becomes visible along with a shadow of the cross. To some, the figure of Jesus seems to move. A little girl seated in front of us excitedly stood up and whispered loudly to her mother, "It's a miracle!" The people at the church don't claim the painting is a miracle, but it is an interesting spectacle.

I believe true miracles have happened and continue to do so. Many miracles Jesus did are reported in the Bible. They are amazing. Many indicate the power Jesus has over the normal processes of nature. Jesus presented others as signs of his messianic nature. The miracles are sometimes referred to as supernatural events. This is often understood as events that happen outside the normal or natural world. Others view miracles as happenings not outside the laws of nature but within and somehow exceeding the laws of nature.

When I spoke about this topic in one of my Bible classes, an older man reported that as a youngster he used to rebuild automobile engines for his hot rod. He called the engine a "souped-up" engine—that is, an engine that would operate in a more superior fashion than an ordinary one. With respect to miracles, he speculated that perhaps Jesus didn't go outside the normal laws of nature; he just souped up the natural laws so the natural laws operated in a faster or super and more superior way. He stayed within the natural laws of nature and just sped them up so they happened instantaneously. I thought his understanding and description of miracles were quite novel, and because I thought his interesting description had a lot of merit, I decided to share it with you.

All the miracles reported in the Bible have their source in God. This was revealed to Moses when God promised to do the wonders and miracles that would persuade Pharaoh to release the Israelites from slavery (Ex. 3:20–21). If not for the miracles at the time of the exodus from Egypt, there wouldn't have been the celebration of the Passover meal and the further development of Judaism. If it weren't for the miracle of the resurrection of Jesus in the New Testament, there would be no Christianity with the celebration of the meal of Holy Communion. Miracles are not only amazing; they are extremely important for Judeo-Christian communities.

Miracles were also important for Jesus in his ministry, especially in his proclamation of the gospel of the kingdom. Jesus said, "The time is fulfilled, and the kingdom of God is at hand; repent and believe in the gospel" (Mark 1:15). Later, the Bible says, "Then he began to denounce the cities where most of his mighty works had been done, because they did not repent" (Matt. 11:20). Apparently from these two passages, the proclamation of the good news of the kingdom included mighty works or miracles, which were intended to encourage repentance and belief.

When Jesus worked miracles, those very miracles were not only intended to encourage repentance and belief; they also served to reveal who he was. We can see this most clearly when we remember the question John the Baptist asked while he was in prison concerning whether Jesus was really the promised savior. The Bible puts it this way: "When John heard in prison what Christ was doing, he sent his disciples to ask him 'Are you the one who was to come, or should we expect someone else?'" This question seems strange to me considering that this is the same John the Baptist who, earlier in his ministry, pointed to Jesus and announced his messianic identity by calling him "the Lamb of God, who takes away the sin of the world (John 1:29)." Perhaps we are all a little like John the Baptist; although we know Jesus is our Savior", we, too, go through times when we need the assurance and strengthening of our faith. Jesus provided him that assurance when he reminded John of the many miracles Jesus done.

Jesus said, "Go and tell John what you hear and see: the blind receive their sight and the lame walk, lepers are cleansed and the deaf hear, and the dead are raised up, and the poor have good news preached to them. And blessed is the one who is not offended by me" (Matt. 11:4–6).

The answer Jesus gave is reminiscent of the messianic passage in Isaiah 35:5–6, which says, "Then the eyes of the blind shall be opened, and the ears of the deaf unstopped; then shall the lame man leap like a deer and the tongue of the mute sing for joy." Jesus read the Isaiah 61:1–2 passage in the synagogue at Nazareth (Luke 4:18–30); this passage identified him as the Messiah who will "bring good news to the poor." Every one of the miracles Jesus referenced gave John the Baptist the assurance that Jesus was truly the One who was to come as the promised Messiah. As we look again at these miracles, we too can be reassured and strengthened in our faith.

THE BLIND RECEIVE THEIR SIGHT

Seeing a man who was born blind, Jesus healed him (John 9:1–41). When the blind man had his sight restored, Jesus proclaimed, "I am the light of the world" (John 9:5). The Bible also reveals, "God is light" (1 John 1:5). Didn't Jesus also in this way indicate that he was the light of the world and God? Speaking to some of the critical Pharisees, Jesus referred to what we might call their spiritual blindness (John 9:35–41). When Jesus referred to the miracle of the blind receiving their sight, he reassured John the Baptist that Jesus was indeed the Messiah who was to come. In documenting this miracle, Jesus reassured us also that he is our Savior. Have we also now received our sight from Jesus to see the light of that important truth? Can we see the bird's nest in the mustard tree?

THE LAME WALK

Jesus reminded John the Baptist that in conducting his ministry, the lame were miraculously being enabled to walk. Isaiah once spoke of the messianic age, saying, "Then shall the lame man leap like a deer" (Isa. 35:6).

The New Testament tells us of only a few individual or specific cases of Jesus healing the lame. The Bible does relate passages that include in passing the miraculous healing of the lame while including the mention of other miraculous healings. One of these instances says,

"And great crowds came to him, bringing with them the lame, the blind, the crippled, the mute and many others, and they put them at his feet, and he healed them, so that the crowd wondered, when they saw the mute speaking, the crippled healthy, the lame walking and the blind seeing. And they glorified the God of Israel" (Matt. 15:30–31). Even in this passage there is little distinction made between those identified as crippled, perhaps with limbs other than the feet or legs incapable of being used, and those identified as lame, perhaps those whose feet or legs were disabled.

There is a case of Jesus healing a paralytic who couldn't walk (Luke 5:17–26). This man was so mobility impaired that his friends brought him to Jesus as he lay on a bed. After Jesus miraculously healed the lame man, Luke says, "And immediately he rose up before them and picked up what he had been lying on and went home, glorifying God" (Luke 5:25–26). He also miraculously healed the paralytic servant of a centurion (Matt. 8:5–13).

One of the indications the prophet Isaiah mentioned is that the messiah, the one to come, would be one who could enable the lame to walk (Isa. 29:18–19; 35:5–6). John was now reminded and reassured that Jesus is the One who fulfilled the words of the prophet.

THE LEPERS ARE CLEANSED

There are numerous mentions of lepers and leprosy in the Bible. The disease identified as leprosy in the Bible covers many skin diseases we know of today. In Bible times it was considered very contagious. Today true leprosy is known as Hansen's disease. It isn't a very contagious disease, although it is communicable; that is, with long-term close contact, it can be communicated to another individual.

It is treated today with antibiotics and other drugs, which weren't available in ancient times. During Old Testament times and at the time of Jesus, lepers were isolated from the public because of the fear of infecting others. If a leper were to come close to another unaffected person, it was necessary to give a warning, such as crying out the words, "Unclean, Unclean!" (Lev. 13:45). A leper had to contend not only with the disease but also with the isolation from friends and family together with the rejection of the general society. If someone with leprosy in Bible times was thought to be cured, which was rare, it was necessary to present oneself to the priests to verify the cure.

At one time ten lepers shouted at him saying, "'Jesus, Master, have mercy on us.' When he saw them he said to them, 'Go show yourselves to the priests.' And as they went they were cleansed" (Luke 17:13–14).

There is another incident when a leper came to Jesus, saying, "'Lord, if you will, you can make me clean.' And Jesus stretched out his hand and touched him, saying, 'I will; be clean.' And immediately his leprosy was cleansed" (Matt. 8:2–3). The one thing I especially like about this miracle of the cleansing of a leper is that it says Jesus touched him. Jesus *touched* him! No one in those days would touch a leper. A leper was considered ritually unclean, and anyone who touched such a person was also considered unclean until he or she underwent a ritually cleansing process. That Jesus touched this leper indicates his great compassion, acceptance, and love for such a person, or for that matter anyone who wasn't acceptable for inclusion in what was then considered the proper and respectable society.

John the Baptist was in prison. Even before his imprisonment, the temple establishment at Jerusalem considered him outside the norm for a faithful Israelite. No doubt some of the temple establishment marked him as an anti- or counter-temple heretical preacher. For John to be reminded that Jesus touched a leper and miraculously healed him must have reassured him that Jesus not only was the promised One but also still loved him since he was also an outcast, suffering isolation from family, friends, and his believing community while being ostracized as a convicted prisoner.

THE DEAF HEAR

When I was a seminarian, I became acquainted with another seminarian who was deaf. There were several other students who knew American Sign Language and were his friends. In time I became able to learn some elementary sign language. One Sunday I was invited to attend a church for the deaf and hearing impaired. As I was being shown the Sunday school rooms, I was very interested because the church where I had grown up had offered a Christian day school but no Sunday school. I had never attended a Sunday school class. Suddenly I was told that one small class had no teacher for this Sunday and that I was the only one who could be available to teach those children using American Sign Language. I felt sorry for those little children, and at the same time, I was quite petrified. But it was one of those offers I couldn't refuse.

After teaching the Sunday school class the best I could, I was introduced to a man who was both blind and deaf. He would lightly hold his hands over mine so he could feel the words I was spelling. To me this ability was absolutely amazing. I was later told about another blind and deaf person who was once asked why he attended church if he could neither see nor hear. His answer was that this was one way he could witness to others whose side he was on.

There is an account in the Bible that tells us about Jesus miraculously healing a deaf man. "And they brought to him a man who was deaf and had a speech impediment, and they begged him to lay his hand on him. And taking him aside from the crowd privately he put his fingers into his ears, and after spitting touched his tongue. And looking up to heaven, he sighed and said to him, '*Ephphatha*,' that is, 'Be opened.' And his ears were opened, his tongue was released, and he spoke plainly" (Mark 7:32–36).

When John the Baptist heard of such miracles Jesus did, surely his faith was strengthened in the truth that Jesus was indeed the messiah who was to come. As Jesus said, "If anyone has ears to hear, let him hear" (Mark 4:23).

THE POOR HAVE GOOD NEWS PREACHED TO THEM

Jesus considered his calling to proclaim the good news of the kingdom. When he was in Capernaum, his good messages were so well received that when he wanted to leave, they wanted him to stay longer. He said to them, "I must preach the good news of the kingdom of God to the other towns as well; for I was sent for this purpose" (Luke 4:43). Many lacked the comfort and blessings of the good news Jesus proclaimed. In that sense, they were spiritually poor and needed the richness of his good news. Certainly the poor were also those who lacked any abundance of material necessities, but when they heard the good news of the kingdom, which Jesus gave to them, they received the riches of faith, hope, and love needed to persevere. The poor were lifted and built up in their faith, as they heard Jesus say in one of his beatitudes. "Blessed are the poor in spirit, for theirs is the kingdom of heaven" (Matt. 5:3). As Jesus came to them, the poor received the kingdom of heaven, and they became joyfully rich beyond all measure. Proclaiming the good news to the poor was a clear messianic sign that Jesus was indeed the One who was to come. When John the Baptist asked about the messianic identity of Jesus, this was an indication of John's poverty of a confident faith while he suffered imprisonment. As John received the message of Jesus, he too was able to rejoice in the richness of the kingdom Jesus proclaimed. In doing so Jesus fulfilled his messianic purpose on earth of bringing the kingdom of heaven to the poor (Isa. 61:1; Luke 4:1).

THE DEAD ARE RAISED

Our common experience about life and death is that some find it extremely difficult to accept the claims of anyone rising from the dead. Medical science has seen considerable advances, so much so that we have become familiar with reports of people being resuscitated from apparent clinical death. It is probably good at this point to make a distinction between the terms *resuscitation* and *resurrection*. Resuscitation is a process that brings someone back from a deathly condition to what we recognize as conscious life. Resurrection is the process of being restored from death to life. The term *resurrection* is used especially for the resurrection of Jesus from death. With respect to the resurrection of Jesus, I like to think of resurrection as rising from death to life without dying again. Resuscitation is rising from death to life only at some time later to die again. I'm aware that the word *resurrection* is at times also used for resuscitation. I prefer that the term *resurrection* refers only to the resurrection of Jesus and the resurrection of the dead at the last day.

When the subject of death is part of the discussion, many ask about near-death experiences. There are numerous reports and books about this subject. One of the first books on near-death experiences I became aware of was written by Dr. Raymond Moody Jr., which raised the awareness of many about these experiences.[1] Most of the experiences related were positive experiences. Since then many books have been written about visits to heaven. Another book by Dr. Maurice Rawlings[2] includes positive near-death experiences, but his research also includes those negative ones about hell.

There is also now much discussion about what actually accounts for death. Is death simply the cessation of the vital signs, such as the beating of the heart and breathing? Is it the cessation of brain activity? When does death actually occur? We are at a time in history when one's body can be kept at a certain stage of functioning, even after what is commonly understood as death has taken place. It is good for medical science to continue the investigation into what might be understood to serve as a standard definition of death.

What is my opinion of near-death accounts? When I worked on call as a hospice chaplain, I became more aware of such experiences. I cannot say people don't have these experiences, but I cannot declare that all these interesting events prove the existence of either heaven or hell. The proof of heaven and hell doesn't rest on the reports of near-death experiences. Proof of heaven and hell rests only upon the biblical accounts.

When John the Baptist sought the answer to whether Jesus was the Messiah, he was told that among the many miracles Jesus did was that he raised the dead. The Bible tells us he raised a young man from the dead in the village of Nain (Luke 7:11–17). Jesus also raised a young girl from the dead who was the daughter of Jairus, a ruler of the synagogue (Mark 5:35–43). In addition, he raised Lazarus of

Bethany from the dead. After Jesus raised Lazarus from the dead, the temple establishment heard what he had done.

> So the chief priests and the Pharisees gathered the Council and said, "What are we to do? For this man performs many signs. If we let him go on like this, everyone will believe in him, and the Romans will come and take away both our place and our nation." But one of them, Caiaphas, who was high priest that year said to them, "You know nothing at all. Nor do you understand that it is better for you that one man should die for the people, not that the whole nation should perish." He did not say this of his own accord, but being high priest that year he prophesied that Jesus would die for the nation, and not for the nation only, but also to gather into one the children of God who are scattered abroad. So from that day on they made plans to put him to death. (John 11:47–53)

Jesus appealed to many miracles he had done to assure John the Baptist that he was the promised messiah. When listing the different miracles, I see that the one that is most notable and caused the most concern among the temple establishment was the raising of people from the dead. When Jesus read the passage from chapter sixty-one of the prophet Isaiah in the synagogue at Nazareth, he declared that he was the fulfillment of this messianic passage. Although the Isaiah passage does mention other messianic indicators, it doesn't include the raising of the dead.

In Jerusalem, there is a museum called the Shrine of the Book. This museum houses many items connected with the discovery of

the Dead Sea Scrolls at Qumran. One of the scrolls discovered is
the scroll of the book of Isaiah. A facsimile of the Isaiah scroll is
prominently displayed in the museum. The Isaiah scroll is important
because it reflects the remarkable accuracy of our present translations
with the ancient scrolls found at Qumran.

Regarding the Dead Sea Scrolls, there is a finding that seems to
have an association with the Isaiah scrolls and the Luke 7 passage
concerning John the Baptist's question about the messianic identity
of Jesus. The finding of this is a scroll that is suggested to be from
part of the Q, or source, and which may have played a part in
construction of the Gospels according to Matthew and Luke.[3] This
scroll portion clearly mentions the raising of the dead and in this
way plays a significant part in messianic identification. This scroll
is numbered 4Q521.[4]

The Dead Sea Scrolls date prior to the time of Jesus. To me it seems
likely that the scholars among the temple establishment were also
aware of information like this concerning the raising of the dead
and its messianic implications. Many others held such expectations
of the promised messiah at this time. The messianic connection of
this reference would of course link to the miracles of Jesus's raising
of the dead and would have caused the temple establishment much
distress. Their distress at the raising of Lazarus from the dead was
great enough to cause their sinister reaction of plotting the death of
Jesus (John 11:53).

It may have also been possible for John the Baptist himself to have
been aware of this Dead Sea Scroll and its mention of the raising
of the dead with its messianic connection. Whether he was aware
of this scroll, the many miracles Jesus listed are more than enough
to assure John that Jesus was indeed the One who was to come, the

promised Messiah. The apostle Peter spoke on the day of Pentecost after the resurrection of Jesus to people gathered in Jerusalem (Acts 2:25–28). He indicated that the resurrection of Jesus the Messiah was the fulfillment of Psalm 16:8–11.

Regarding the messiah and the raising of the dead, I cannot leave this subject without mentioning the greatest miracle of all, the resurrection of Jesus from the dead. Although this event occurred after the death of John the Baptist, it is a miracle that validates the messianic identity of Jesus together with all he taught and accomplished for the sake of his faithful followers until the present day.

All the synoptic gospels plus the Gospel according to John tell of the resurrection of Jesus from the dead. The very earliest mention of the resurrection of Jesus, however, occurs not in the Gospels but in 1 Corinthians 15. The letter to the Corinthians was written around AD 55, which may have been somewhat earlier than the other Gospels were written. When compared to many other accounts of ancient historical happenings, the Corinthians account and the Gospel accounts of the resurrection of Jesus are written much closer to the original happening than many other writings about ancient historical events. This in itself lends credence to the authenticity of the resurrection. In addition to the resurrection of Jesus itself, the letter to the Corinthians lists the large number of visual sightings of the risen Christ, verifying Jesus's rising to life again after his death and the validity of his life and teachings (1 Cor. 15:3–8).

After the resurrection of Jesus and the empowerment by the Holy Spirit of his followers at Pentecost, the disciples went out to proclaim the resurrection and its meaning to people throughout the then-known world. They did this, even though the prevailing dangerous governmental anti-Christian persecutions placed them in a position to lose their lives. Would you put your lives at risk to proclaim the risen Christ in such a dangerous world if you weren't perfectly certain Jesus had actually risen from the dead? The apostle Paul put it very clearly for Christians at that time and for now when he wrote, "And if Christ has not been raised, your faith is futile and you are still in your sins. Then those also who have fallen asleep in Christ have perished. If in this life only we have hoped in Christ, we are of all people most to be pitied … But in fact Christ has been raised from the dead, the firstfruits of those who have fallen asleep" (1 Cor. 15:17–20).

The resurrection of Jesus is of great importance for everyone. Because Jesus rose from the dead, we have the assurance that everything he taught is true. All he did, especially his death on the cross, is validated by his resurrection as a perfect sacrifice for everyone, so all are saved from eternal death and for life everlasting in heaven. His resurrection brings us a complete life now and a perfect life after death, which is a marvelous blessing to each of us. While Jesus was speaking with his disciples at the Last Supper, and before his sacerdotal prayer, he assured his disciples, saying, "Because I live, you also will live" (John 14:19). Because Jesus rose from the dead, his resurrection brings life to all who put their trust in him. This is very good news for me. I can trust him every day of my life here on earth for all I need and for a happy and joyous life with him, even after my death. This reminds me of what Job said about his faith in a personal resurrection. "For I know that my Redeemer lives, and at the last he will stand upon the earth. And after my skin has been thus destroyed, yet in my flesh I shall see God, whom I shall see for myself, and my eyes shall behold, and not another. My heart faints within me!" (Job 19: 25-27). It's almost like Job is saying, "I can see the bird's nest in the mustard tree!"

Every Easter all who trust in him celebrate the miracle of his resurrection together with all the happy and joyous blessings it brings to everyone. The resurrection of Jesus brings the gospel of his kingdom into our lives as a validated and certain reality. Can you see the bird's nest in my mustard tree?

Chapter 10

AN APOCALYPTIC
PROCLAMATION?

Was Jesus's proclamation of the gospel of the kingdom an apocalyptic message? When the word *apocalyptic* or *apocalypse* is used, many people think of terrible happenings, including doom and destruction approaching the end of all things. First, let's refresh our memories about what the term *apocalyptic* actually means. The Greek word translated *apocalypse* simply means to unveil or to reveal that which what was concealed. Sometimes the book of the Revelation to John is referred to as the Apocalypse to John. The terms *revelation* and *apocalypse* simply mean the same thing and refer to something being disclosed or revealed. The book of Revelation begins by telling us that it is "the revelation of Jesus Christ, which God gave him to show to his servants the things that must soon take place" (Rev. 1:1).

The book of the Revelation to John was written in a certain literary style called "apocalyptic literature." There are other examples of this literary style in the Hebrew Bible, in parts of the books of Daniel and Ezekiel, and in a few shorter examples in the New Testament that were written in the apocalyptic style. Briefly, apocalyptic messages were messages of hope, stating that the faithful should stand firm in the faith because God will soon deliver. "Be faithful unto death, and I will give you the crown of life" (Rev. 2:10).

But the question remains. Was the proclamation of the gospel of the kingdom by Jesus an apocalyptic message? The claim is often stated that Jesus was an apocalyptic preacher and that his message was a message about terrible times that are coming: repent for the end is near. Then all hopes of the faithful will be fulfilled near the time when all things finally end. The message of Jesus certainly was a message extending hope pertaining to the kingdom he proclaimed. People who are by faith in his kingdom can experience hope during this life and into eternity. That is certainly a message of good news or gospel. It is a gospel of the kingdom message, which doesn't exclusively attach itself to the coming of God at the end of time for the faithful to be delivered from their difficulties and ushered into his kingdom. It is a kingdom that can actually be experienced during one's life in the present time and in addition extend in time even to those living until the last day. It is apocalyptic in the sense that it reveals that God intervenes in our lives with all its conditions and circumstances, and delivers us from what is dangerous or difficult for us. He does this in his own way and time.

There are some who think of Jesus's proclamation as apocalyptic because it refers to a message that offers the kingdom as coming into fruition for the people only when God returns shortly or finally at the end of time. The kingdom referred to is the kingdom many envision as a restored military, political, and geographical kingdom like that of David and Solomon or even like the Hasmonean kingdom the Maccabean Revolt against Syrian rule brought into being. The many oppressed people under foreign pagan powers, such as the Roman Empire, longed to be delivered into such a kingdom. The apocalyptic message, then, is simply that we should hold fast to looking forward to the coming of God at a time thought to be soon, but if not, it will take place at the end of time, and then we will be rescued or delivered from our miserable existence and granted entrance into God's glorious utopian-like kingdom. Such an understanding of an apocalyptic message is more of a "this-world" or even an End Times or eschatologically oriented message rather than the gospel of the kingdom Jesus actually proclaimed.

I don't believe a person needs to wait for God to come so that he might deliver us into his kingdom at the end of time or revolt against the earthly powers. I believe that to be delivered isn't that one must wait until Jesus comes at the End Times for us to be delivered. The reality is that God has already come in the person of Jesus, and we are already delivered and participating in his kingdom. This is the gospel of the kingdom Jesus proclaimed. It is the message Jesus revealed. In that sense, it can perhaps be called an "apocalyptic" or "revealed message."

The gospel of the kingdom is a good news message that celebrates the fact that the King has already come into our lives in the person of Jesus Christ. We now experience both sorrows and joys, but we experience them in his active and loving presence. He has come into our lives and is daily and actively present with us so we might be continually delivered from evil. We can now forever experience the joyous multitude of the blessings available in his kingdom. Jesus was, he is, and he is to come. He is the alpha and omega, and so is the gospel of the kingdom. That is the so-called mysterious gospel or good news of the kingdom that is no longer so mysterious. It is the good news of the kingdom Jesus has revealed to us in his proclamations of word and deed during his earthly mission and ministry. Can you see the bird's nest in my mustard tree?

A RECAPITULATION

In the beginning of our search for the meaning of the gospel or good news of the kingdom Jesus proclaimed, we had hoped to gain a fuller understanding of what it was that comprised the gospel of the kingdom. We reviewed what the kingdom meant to the people of Jesus's day and what Jesus might have meant by the kingdom. The concept of presence then became important in our inquiry and more specifically as it relates to Jesus himself as being actively present with us. I was particularly impressed with the many stories or parables Jesus used to give us a glimpse into the many facets of what the gospel of the kingdom is. We broadened our understanding of the kingdom by pointing out the multidimensional quality of the kingdom.

All kingdoms have laws. The gospel of the kingdom Jesus proclaims gives us a new commandment: that we should love one another as Jesus has loved us. The gospel of the kingdom is the good news of God's active love for us. There is no elite class that excludes others in the gospel of the kingdom Jesus preached. He and his kingdom are for everyone. Jesus is for all ordinary people. We are all among the ordinary people. There are no class distinctions. His kingdom is, however, an extraordinary kingdom that includes the Messiah's intervention into our lives through healings and miracles. In the end, we reviewed the pros and cons of whether Jesus was an apocalyptic preacher and discovered he is timeless, the alpha and omega, the beginning and the end, always present to deliver us from evil.

The whole of what the gospel of the kingdom is began to become more apparent as we presented the various facets of the kingdom. In combining these various insights, the gospel of the kingdom has become so intimately identified with Jesus that the gospel of the kingdom and Jesus have, for all practical purposes, become one.

Throughout this inquiry, I have occasionally used the question "Can you see the bird's nest in my mustard tree?" I have used this literary device as a reminder that it isn't always so easy to recognize the various seemingly inconspicuous aspects related to Jesus and the mysterious gospel of the kingdom. When we take a closer look, however, the complete and real picture of the gospel of the kingdom begins to emerge for us to see.

MAKING IT PERSONAL

The gospel of the kingdom isn't just a historical proclamation Jesus declared for the people over two thousand years ago. It speaks to me personally today. I rejoice that Jesus by grace brought me into his kingdom so I might receive the many blessings of being a citizen of his dominion simply by trusting in him. I'm happy to be joined together with all others throughout the world who also trust in him. Jesus is the center of my life. He is actively present and constantly loves, forgives, and strengthens me through his word and sacraments.

I find the world around me, which he created, beautifully uplifting and filled with his loving care. His multidimensional kingdom abounds with his wonder and presents me with discoveries yet to be enjoyed. With Jesus, there is life and life abundant. With Jesus as the ruler of his kingdom, I feel confident, trusting his control over me and his dominion over all things. I trust Jesus with my life now and for his gracious gift of everlasting salvation for my whole being, even after death. That's the gospel, the good news, Jesus proclaimed years ago, and with that he actively and personally gifts me today. As you also trust Jesus during your life, may your experience with him in his kingdom be as great a blessing for you as it has continually blessed me. Can you see the bird's nest in my mustard tree?

THE DOXOLOGY

The Lord's Prayer, as written in the New Testament (Matt. 6:9–13), doesn't include the doxology, which for many Christians is the familiar ending of the prayer. The doxology includes the words "For yours is the kingdom and the power and the glory, forever. Amen." There are some old manuscripts of the Bible that do include the familiar doxology. Those who use the King James Version of the Bible will see that the doxology is included. I grew up using the popular King James Version of the Bible and was shocked to discover that some of the newer versions of the Bible don't include the doxology. It was then that I became aware that some more reliable ancient manuscripts have been discovered since the King James Version was written and that these manuscripts don't include those words. This is why it isn't included in the more recent Bible translations.

The doxology to the Lord's Prayer, however, remains a beautiful, traditional ending for the prayer, and many Christian churches still use it in their worship services. I like the doxology. It serves as an especially good reminder regarding some important truths we have reviewed in researching the gospel of the kingdom, which Jesus proclaimed and which has been the focus of our inquiry.

In the Lord's Prayer, he began by saying, "Our Father in heaven, hallowed by your name. Your kingdom come, your will be done, on earth as it is in heaven." When he mentioned the kingdom, notice that he said, "Your kingdom come." So the question is, is it the Father's kingdom or Jesus's kingdom? Jesus gave us the answer when his disciple Philip asked, "'Lord, show us the Father, and it is enough for us.' Jesus said to him, 'Have I been with you so long, and you still do not know me, Philip? Whoever has seen me has seen the father. How can you say, 'Show us the Father'? Do you not believe that I am in the Father and the Father is in me?'" (John 14:8–9). There is no separation here. It can be called the "kingdom of the Father" or the "kingdom of Jesus."

It is a kingdom that belongs to our Father, a kingdom that belongs to Jesus. It isn't a kingdom we create. It isn't something we own. It isn't the earthly church. The church has been given the means, the word, and the sacraments through which we receive God's grace. It is through those means of grace that God works to bring people into his kingdom, but the kingdom itself isn't something we construct on our own. How humbling! Yet it is a great privilege for each of us in the church to extend his good news through the means of grace and through which God works so wondrously to receive people into his kingdom. When we pray that God's kingdom come, we pray that it may be extended to all who are not yet in his kingdom. It is a mission prayer.

Notice also that the doxology, in addition to attributing the kingdom to God, also attributes power to God. This is important for all to acknowledge as we speak the doxology. We are not the Almighty. All power belongs to him. Unfortunately, it seems that we, his people, are tempted all too often to selfishly use power for ourselves. Too often we are tempted to use power to control others. Whether this control takes place in our personal relationships or even within the earthly church organization itself, God forbid; power belongs to

God and we should not try to steal that power to obtain our own selfish ends.

At the very beginning of his earthly ministry, Jesus didn't always and fully exercise his divine power to accomplish his saving mission. When the devil tempted Jesus to use his power to turn stones into bread to satisfy his intense hunger after fasting, he refused the devil's temptation to use his almighty power in this way, saying, "It is written, 'Man shall not live by bread alone, but by every word that comes from the mouth of God'" (Matt. 3:4). It would be much better for us to resist the temptation as Jesus did to use power to satisfy our personal desires and ambitions. We can instead strive to search for ways to humbly love and serve people so a right result can be obtained.

The doxology then says, "For yours is the … glory." All glory belongs to God. In the doxology, we ascribe to God the highest honor possible. The very word *doxology* is derived from two Greek words, *doxa* and *logos. Doxa* is translated as glory or praise. *Logos* is translated as word. The term doxology can be translated as "words of glory" or "words of praise." He is the One who deserves to receive such an exalted distinction of honor and glory. People who excel in sports, the various arts, and other professions are often recognized for their accomplishments by being given special awards and honors. Such honors and recognition attach a certain amount of praise and glory to the recipient, but compared to the highest honor and glory ascribed to God such human honor and glory are dull and fleeting. In the doxology, we offer God all the greatness, glory, majesty, and exaltation he deserves.

The doxology concludes with the word *amen.* So often when people hear this word, they simply think it means the speech, address, or prayer has come to an end. The word *amen* is understood to be much like the words *the end* that appear on the screen when a movie is over. Actually the word *amen* indicates the person's assent or agreement with what has been said. The word *amen* is like saying, "Yes" or "So let it be so" to what has been said.

A doxology is not only appropriate to conclude the Lord's Prayer but also appropriate, perhaps even more so, to conclude this inquiry into the gospel of the kingdom Jesus proclaimed. To him be the kingdom, the power, and all the glory. Amen.

Benediction

Go.

Be happy

In being

Yourself,

Becoming

More than you are

Doing,

The loving thing

With

Joy.

Endnotes

CHAPTER 2

1. *The New Oxford Annotated Bible with the Apocrypha/Dueterocanonical Books* (New York: Oxford University Press, 1977). An account of the rebellion against Antiochus IV, Epiphanes, is available in 1 Maccabees. cf. *The Apocrypha, The Lutheran Edition with Notes* (St. Louis: Concordia, 2012), 1 Maccabees.
2. Paul L. Maier, *Josephus: The Essential Works* (Grand Rapids: Kregel, 1994), 280. This provides a brief description of the sicarii.
3. J. I., Packer and M. C. Tenney, eds., *Manners and Customs of the Bible* (Nashville: Thomas Nelson, 1980), 509.
4. Tregelles, Samuel Prideaux, *Gesenius' Hebrew and Chaldee Lexicon to the Old Testament Scriptures, (*Grand Rapids, Michigan, *1954)* *9,191, 514.*

CHAPTER 3

1. Paul Tillich, The Eternal Now (New York: Charles Scribner's Sons, 1963), 16, 24–25.

CHAPTER 4

1. William J. Bennett, ed., The Moral Compass (New York: Simon & Schuster, 1995). This is a collection of stories from numerous sources; the editor calls them "Stories for a Life's Journey."
2. Nicolaus Ludwig von Zinzendorf, *Lutheran Service Book* (St. Louis: Concordia, 2006), 563.

3. Frederick W. Danker, *Jesus and the New Age* (St. Louis: Clayton, 1972), 159, 160.

CHAPTER 5

1. Paul Tillich, The Eternal Now, 500.
2. Paul Davies, *God and the New Physics* (New York: Simon & Schuster, 1983), 100–118. This is an excellent book covering many religious questions from the perspective of an academic physicist.
3. Ian P. McGreal, ed., *Great Thinkers of the Western World* (New York: HarperCollins, 1992), 480.
4. Masaru Emoto, *The Hidden Messages in Water* (New York: Atria Books, 2005). 39. This book contains a number of experiments conducted by Dr. Emoto concerning molecules of water and how they are affected by thoughts, words, and feelings.
5. Ibid., 43.
6. Marvin Meyer, *The Gospel of Thomas: The Hidden Sayings of Jesus* (New York: HarperSanFrancisco, 1992), 23.
7. Ibid., 108.

CHAPTER 6

1. Francis Pieper, Christian Dogmatics, vol. 2 (St. Louis: Concordia, 1951), 403. "Likewise the term repentance (peonitentia, metanoia) denotes in some Scripture passages not only the knowledge of sin, but also faith in the forgiveness of sins (Luke 15:7)."
2. Alan Richardson, ed., *A Theological Word Book of the Bible* (New York: Macmillan, 1971), 131–136.
3. Alfred Rahlfs, ed., *Septuaginta,* vol. 1 (Wurttembergische Bibelanstalt, 1971), xxxII, "History of the Septuaginta text." The Septuaginta uses the word *eros* in its text of Proverbs 7:18.

Chapter 8

1. Bruce E. Schein, Following the Way (Minneapolis: Augsburg, 1980), 86–91.

2. Martin Luther, *Luther's Small Catechism with Explanation* (Concordia, 1986), 29. "The Benefit of the Sacrament of the Altar: 'These words, "Given and shed for you for the forgiveness of sins," show us that in the Sacrament forgiveness of sins, life, and salvation are given us through these words. For where there is forgiveness of sins, there is also life and salvation.'"

Chapter 9

1. Raymond A. Moody Jr., M.D., Life after Life (New York: Bantam Books, 1976). This book documents a number of a physician's observations concerning patients reporting near death experiences especially of heaven.

2. Maurice Rawlings, M.D., *Beyond Death's Door* (Nashville: Thomas Nelson, 1978). This book documents a physician's observation of a number of patient's near death experiences including those of being in hell.

3. Bas Library, Biblical Archaeology Society Dead Sea Scrolls Counsel: fragments, "The Messiah text: 4Q521 and a line-by-line analysis by Michael O. Wise and James D. Tabor," http:www.qumronscrolls/4Q521/thesigns of the messiah (September 19, 2016).

4. TextExcavation,"QumranScroll4Q521," http://www.textexcavation.com/qumran4Q521 (September 19, 2016), "he will heal the badly wounded and will make the dead live; he will proclaim good news to the poor." Fragment 2. Column 2.

Printed in the United States
By Bookmasters